Illustrated Living History Series

TALL SHIPS
OF THE
WORLD

C. Keith Wilbur

Chelsea House Publishers

Philadelphia

First published in hardback edition in 1997 by Chelsea House Publishers.

1 3 5 7 9 8 6 4 2

Library of Congress Cataloging-in-Publication Data

Wilbur, Keith, 1923-
Tall Ships of the World / C. Keith Wilbur.
p.   cm. -- (Illustrated living history series)
Originally published: Chester, CT: Globe Pequot Press, c1986.
Includes bibliographical references and index.
ISBN 0-7910-4526-9 (hc)
1. Sailing ships. 2. Seafaring life. I. Title. II. Series.
VM145.W55 1997
387.2'2--dc20   96-43017
                                                            CIP

CONTENTS

FOREWORD

The world has recently seen a dramatic increase in interest in tall ships by sailors and nonsailors alike. Tall ships are irresistibly enchanting to people everywhere. Major cities, American and foreign, compete in the effort to entice tall ships to their ports to participate in all kinds of celebrations. Crowds gather along shores for parades of sail as the masts and flags of many nations pass by modern office buildings. People of all ages wait in long lines for the chance to walk the decks, to touch the brass, to gape at the confusion of rigging, or to stand for a moment at the helm. Why are we seeing this enthusiasm for tall ships?

Part of the mystique is due to their being the modern representatives of those familiar names of the past—*Bounty, Victory, Cutty Sark, Pequod,* and all the other warships, whalers, and clippers that have filled our history and our literature with romance and splendor. Sailing ships are so much a part of our common heritage that even those who can't tell a barque from a brig can take pride in what the tall ships represent—one of man's finest efforts at mastering and utilizing the forces of nature. We wonder at the genius of the inventors of early rigging and sail plans. We feel intense admiration for the courage of those brave explorers who dared to sail toward the edge of the Earth where dragons lurked. And we are thankful that, in the winds of the nuclear age, sails still billow, halyards are hauled, and yards are braced.

The tall ships we see today, however, are very different from the creaking, wooden vessels that crossed the oceans of other ages. Most of the Class A tall ships are in fact younger than many of the visitors walking their decks! Steel has replaced wood in hulls and spars. Diesel engines, satellite navigation, and computerized communication systems have become standard. Most quarters are air-conditioned, and most freezers contain ice cream. The scruffy tars of the past, plagued by accidents and disease, have been replaced by healthy young sailors in peak physical condition. No longer used for trading, exploration, whaling, or war, the tall ships are now primarily training vessels.

But why do so many countries use sailing ships to train future officers of power-driven vessels? Tall ships are the most basic of nautical classrooms, yet the complexity of the standing and running rigging and the large number of sails are a problem for even an experienced sailor. Anyone who has seen the look of pride in a cadet's eyes upon completion of a well-executed sail evolution knows that there are still extraordinary challenges available to young people. Most United States Coast Guard officers can claim *Eagle* experience as part of their training because the Coast Guard believes that in learning the fundamental principles of setting sail and utilizing currents, her young officers will develop a keen sense of the vicissitudes of wind and water. The cadet who has climbed a gyrating mast to furl a sail in a storm or has labored at the helm in fifteen-foot waves will never underestimate the power of the sea. The unique contribution of the tall ship today, however, is that it provides an ideal environment of developing leadership, teamwork, endurance, and discipline. In past centuries, the crew's survival depended on their ability to work together toward a common goal. Lives are seldom at risk today, yet the same professional conduct and cooperation are needed to achieve a successful passage.

Though some of us will have the good fortune to sail aboard one of the world's tall ships, most will never get closer than the pages of a book. C. Keith Wilbur's illustrations and detailed facts about tall ship history and traditions will give readers a feeling for the realities of life on board and a deeper understanding of why we continue to have such a fascination for those grand ladies of the sea, the tall ships.

Captain Ernst M. Cummings, USCG
former commanding officer
USCG Barque *Eagle*

INTRODUCTION

Rhode Island's Narragansett Bay gave me my first baptism under sail~if one could call it sailing. Our ancient dory had an inboard motor of dubious heritage. It was an adventure~ and a challenge~ for my brother and me to get that engine to turn over and putter from Quonset Point to our grandmother's cottage down the bay.

One hot summer's day, on our return the engine died. Rather than give it a decent burial at sea, and instead of breaking out the oars for the long haul home, we rigged up a make shift sail from old canvas. It worked~ at least somewhat. We raised no blisters that day, and we were grateful to let the wind move us homeward.

I'd thought of those easy-going days with our jury-rigged sail since~particularly when I was on the bridge of a subchaser during World War II. Our job was to shepherd convoys from England to our beachheads on the French coast and to run down any submarine that might try to send us elsewhere. The choppy English Channel seas didn't mix well with a stern wind that blew diesel stroke into our eyes and lungs. Narragansett Bay seemed very far away with its kinder waters and fume-free wind propulsion.

It wasn't until 1976 that I revisited the bay for one of the most exciting events of the decade. The Tall Ships had come to visit Newport, and, it seemed, all the world was there for a proper welcome. My brother-in-law's lobster boat wove us around and about those graceful beauties. It was enough to take one's breath away and to provide one of life's great memories. But~ landlubber that I was~ there were many questions that I had about those windjammers that sailed out of the past. There seemed to be mighty few answers. Tall Ships of the World, then, may help share with the reader what life would be like aboard our square-riggers ~ past and present.

Since these pages hold only a layman's perspective of the Tall Ships and the men and women who sail them, the reader need not look for a Certificate of Square-Rigged Sailing Proficiency at the end of the book. But further in-depth reading in the bibliography and visits to the marine museums listed might lead to a real sail-training adventure or a career in the United States Coast Guard or Navy.

Few shore-bound girls could compete with the sailor's first love~ the tall ship on which he sailed. Under a sky full of sail, she (for every ship is a she) called the adventurer away from the dust and clutter of the port and out onto the open sea. He knew her well~ from figurehead to her sternboard and from royal to mainsail~ and by his seamanship she came to life. Over the horizon, weather willing, his ship carried him and his crewmates to strange lands and exotic ports. Certainly the seafarer's affection for his graceful island of canvas needed no apologies.

Richard Dana, serving his <u>Two Years Before The Mast</u>, gave a hint of this bond back in 1836. "One night, while we were in these tropics, I went out to the end of the flying-jib-boom, upon some duty and, having finished it, turned round and lay over the boom for half an hour, admiring the beauty of the sight before me. Being so far out from the deck, I could look at the ship as a separate vessel;~ and there, rose up from the water, supported only by the small black hull, a pyramid of canvass, spreading out far beyond the hull and towering up almost, as it seemed in the indistinct night air, to the clouds. The sea was as still as an inland lake; the light trade-wind was gently and steadily breathing from astern; the dark blue sky was studded with the tropical stars; there was not a sound but the rippling of the water under the stem; and the sails were spread out, wide and high;~ the two lower studding-sails stretching out on each side, twenty or thirty feet beyond the deck; the top-mast studding-sails, like wings to the top-sails; the top-gallant studding-sails spreading fearlessly out above them; still higher, the two royal studding sails, looking like two kites flying from the same string; and, highest of all, the little sky-sail, the apex of the pyramid, seemed actually to touch the stars, and to be out of reach of human hand. So quiet, too, was the sea, and so steady the breeze, that if these sails had been sculptured marble they could not have been more motionless. Not a ripple upon the surface of the canvass; not even a quivering of the extreme edges of the sail~ so perfectly were they distended by the breeze. I was so lost in the sight, that I forgot the presence of the man who came out with me, until he said, (for he, too, rough old man-of-war's-man as he was, had been gazing at the show,) half to himself, still looking at the marble sails~ 'How quietly they do their work!'"

Dana's ship was a tall ship~ and that term deserves some explanation. As far as the old sailing hands were concerned, to be tall a ship must be a large square-rigged sailer carrying three or more masts. A landlubber by the name of Webster agrees with them. After all, only square sails that extended from side to side could be hung from great heights. Fore-and-aft sails could reach skyward just so far before their booms would run afoul of neighboring masts and rigging.

If a square-rigger is to fill the sky with canvas, its towering masts must be secured to a stable, well-designed hull.

30-INCH FIGUREHEAD OF BRIG OWNER'S DAUGHTER, CLARISSA ANN.

(MAINE MARINE MUSEUM, BATH)

BRIG CLARISSA ANN BATH 1824

SHIP HULLS

When planning the merchantman's hull, cargo and passenger space were prime considerations. In addition, her planked skin must give the least water resistance and yet provide the best possible buoyancy. The three to five foot half-hull models helped translate the designer's ideas into a three-dimensional miniature of the real thing. And half a model was as good as a whole, since both sides of the ship must certainly match.

From the earliest days of the eighteenth century, the American hawksnest model was favored over the solid wood half or full model. The shaping and positioning of the ribs well as the run of its planking (battens) could be measured and drawn to scale for the actual building.

HAWKSNEST MODEL OF REVOLUTIONARY WAR PRIVATEER "DASH" FROM MAINE (B.H. BARTOL LIBRARY, FREEPORT, MAINE)

After the Revolution, half-hull waterline models became the rule. This American innovation was made with alternating cedar and pine boards, sandwiched with dowels into a single block. When whittled to shape, the dark and light contrast lines would run parallel to the water's surface or the keel. In any event, the waterline models simplified the transfer of the pattern to full-sized templates in the mould loft.

Donald McKay was probably the best-known designer of sleek clipper ships. His historic half-models were stored in a barn after his death~only to be chopped up for firewood! Sadly, only three models remain as examples of his Yankee ingenuity. One, the

HALF-HULL WATERLINE MODEL OF THE CLIPPER SHIP "STAGHOUND" SCALE = 4 FEET TO THE INCH TO MAKE WATER LINES 2½ FEET APART. (BOSTON MARINE MUSEUM)

"Staghound," was discovered quite by chance under some old canvas in a local sail loft!

These clipper half-models were in striking contrast to the old bulky and buoyant merchantmen that carried their profitable cargoes. With bottoms nearly as flat as a sea biscuit, there was room and stability aplenty. Unfortunately, they were about as maneuverable as a half a watermelon afloat. The rounded bows were no help, for the waves were pushed aside rather than sliced through. There was a better way, and the evolving hulls of the BALTIMORE CLIPPER, PACKET, EXTREME CLIPPER, and the MODERATE CLIPPER brought about an efficient combination of cargo space and speed. The tall ships of today are the result of these improvements.

BALTIMORE CLIPPER
1820~1860

The Revolution and the War of 1812 had placed a premium on swift sailing. Since the young American navy could offer little if any protection, only a small fast ship could out-run and out-maneuver the British coastal blockade. Privateers were soon tearing

around the Atlantic, cutting out any plump and lumbering stragglers from their convoys. With a few post-war improvements, fleet little vessels ~ rarely over one hundred feet in length ~ were being launched from the countless small shipyards that peppered the Chesapeake Bay area. By their sharp lines, they were known as Baltimore Clippers.

CARVED WOODEN SACRED COD OF MASSACHUSETTS, 1773, NOW HANGING IN THE HOUSE OF REPRESENTATIVES, STATE HOUSE, BOSTON.

That part of the hull underwater was streamlined after the codfish. Although the bow was still rounded below the waterline, it "V'd down to part the waves. The greatest beam or width was well forward, as was the cod's body, giving the little clipper a buoyancy that rode the bow up on the water, much like a surfboard. Her smooth lines tapered aft, as with the fish's tail, to give a thin, deep keel for stability and little water resistance. Indeed, the keel below the bow was only half as deep as at the rudder.

The lines were clean and low above the waterline. Aloft, the two raked masts carried a schooner rig or an occasional brig or brigantine rig. Her swift passages were the talk of European nations, and they were quick to copy her lines for their own. Admittedly the little clipper was no tall ship, but her sharp hull lines were appreciated by the designers of the later fast clipper packets and the tallest of the tall, the extreme clipper.

THE "PRIDE OF BALTIMORE," A REPLICA OF A TYPICAL BALTIMORE CLIPPER, WAS LAUNCHED AT BALTIMORE IN 1977.

"PRIDE OF BALTIMORE"

PACKET HULLS 1820~1857

Peace had freed the seas after the War of 1812. The North Atlantic was fair game for a new breed of vessels that specialized in the delivery of both passengers and cargo on a prearranged schedule to advertised ports. No longer was the sailing date dependent on enough cargo to fill the hold. These were the packets ~ the first ocean liners. Passage from Liverpool to New York averaged about thirty-four days, and thanks to westerly tail winds, the return took but twenty days. It was a reliable ~ almost luxurious ~ way to travel and to ship goods. With crack American officers driving their crews to the limit, our country dominated the profitable packet trade from the outset.

After the flashy days of the Baltimore Clipper, the packet of 1000 to 1500 tons* seemed something of an anticlimax. The high straight sides and bottom as flat as a ship's logbook resembled the tubby frigates of earlier years ~ but they could be loaded to the scuppers. No "V"-shaped clipper hull could approach such capacity. Even the packet bow was rounded and the stern squared to give its load added buoyancy and stability in the heavy Atlantic seas.

* TONNAGE = THE CAPACITY OF A MERCHANT SHIP IN UNITS OF 100 CUBIC FEET.

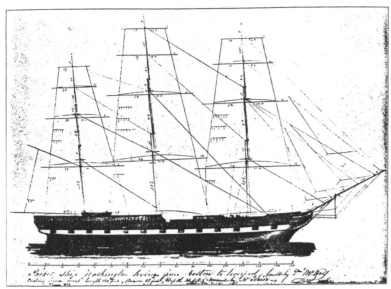

PACKET SHIP "WASHINGTON IRVING," 751 TONS, EAST BOSTON 1845.
(FROM DRAWING BY DONALD McKAY AT THE PEABODY MUSEUM, SALEM.

It was quite a different story below the waterline. There, the bow was sharpened in a modified clipper fashion to cut through the water and not simply punch through it. All in all, the packet was a dry sailer and a comfortable enough vessel, regardless of weather or press of sails that hurried her along.

There was no room allotted for waste space. The raised after end (poop deck) housed the master and his officers while the crew was quartered in the forward deck house (forecastle). The main deck between these "houses" held the life-boats ~ and shelters enough for a small farm. The tired menu of salt meats was relieved with chickens and fresh eggs, and the cow offered milk if sea sickness didn't dry her out. The production problem was solved by generous rations of beer ! There were pigs and geese. Goats were a favorite, for they had sea legs and served as portable disposal units by devouring everything from wood shavings to old news-papers and log books.

The lower deck aft was divided into first-class passenger cabins. The paneled walls of exotic woods, embellished with gold leaf, gave a touch of luxury for the affluent who could afford the one-hundred-and-twenty-five-dollar passage. Forward, with like attention to comfort, was the dining saloon. The kitchen and pantries were beyond, while amidships to the bow was the notorious steerage section for those of lesser means ~ the emigrants.

Increasing competition from the steamships made speed as important as cargo space. Many older and slower packets were sold to the whalers, who found the roomi-ness much to their liking.

CLIPPER PACKET SHIP "RACER" OF NEW YORK.
(FROM WOOD ENGRAVING IN THE ILLUSTRATED LONDON NEWS, OCT. 18, 1851)

The ends became sharpened, and by the 1840s they began to resemble the profile of that fleetest of ships, the American clipper. It was an admirable, all-round tall ship.

THE "CHARLES W. MORGAN," BUILT IN NEW BEDFORD IN 1841, IS THE OLDEST SURVIVING WOODEN AMERICAN WHALER, NOW DOCKED AT MYSTIC SEAPORT, CONNᵀ.

EXTREME CLIPPER HULLS 1841~1860

Back in 1833, few raised their eyebrows when "Ann McKim" was launched at Baltimore. It was not surprising that she was built with Baltimore clipper sharpness, but not to be overlooked were her 493 tons~a large vessel for those days~and ship-rigged as well. Marine architect John W. Griffiths was impressed, however, and eight years later made public a perfected model of the future extreme Yankee clipper ship.

The long and curved bow and the "V" bottomed hull were there. Innovations included a length of considerably greater proportion than her width and an increased underwater depth that made for remarkable stability in high seas. The clippers that followed the drawing board frequently were between 1800 and 2500 tons. There was a graceful deck curve that ran from stem to stern. In Baltimore fashion, the masts were raked aft, giving the impression that she was about to leap over the waves. Indeed, the clipper's towering masts carried such a spread of canvas that she seemed to do just that. She was the tallest of tall with her skysails over her royals and moonsails over the skysails. In all the history of sail, none could equal her record runs.

Master ship-builders such as Donald McKay and William Webb were soon turning out these classics in record numbers. Great Britain's lumbering cargo vessels had long dominated the China tea trade, each competing to bring back the much-sought first crop of the season. However, a slow passage might well mean that a hold filled with tea, spices, and dried fruits could turn to worthless mush. The Yankee clipper~soon known as the China or California clipper~took over this bonanza with ease. In 1852, the "Witch of the Wave"

CLIPPER SHIP "GREAT REPUBLIC" BY DONALD MCKAY   (CURRIER LITHOGRAPH, 1853)

tore from the Orient to England in a record ninety days.

They were ready for the '49 California gold rush as well, racing both men and cargo around Cape Horn to the boom towns. Then it was off to China and back to complete a voyage that could pay for the vessel itself. As for the Atlantic run, they could whisk by both packets and steamers to trim the passage to eighteen days from east to west and fourteen days on the return. Landlubber and sailor alike could share a real affection for a ship such as this.

The Yankee clipper was not without problems. In heavy seas, she was a wet ship with decks constantly awash. Her knife-like bow sliced deeply into the waves rather than riding on the surface. It took a large crew to manage her great heights of canvas under such conditions. Even in those days of high freight charges, wages and cargo space lost to living quarters could make sizable dents in the profits. Most important, the extreme clipper was a swift-sailing specialist in small and valuable cargo. All too soon, her colorful history ended in the face of vanishing markets and steamship competition.

MEDIUM CLIPPER HULLS 1854~1891

Donald McKay, although saddened by the extreme clipper's fall from glory and his own idle shipyard, was not about to let the steamship rule the seas. He reasoned that the best qualities of the packet and the clipper could be combined into an economically sound sailer. His new brainchild was known as the medium clipper~not unlike the last of the sharp-modeled packets. Her relatively flat bottom, as well as an increased length and width, gave a similar buoyancy and stability. The sharp scoop of the bow and fine sternline and the gentle curve of the deckline were borrowed from the clipper.

Although the medium clipper's three masts carried less canvas than her predecessor, she could move a massive amount of cargo down the sea lanes at a very respectable rate. Here was a handsome tall ship that handled as well as she looked. When bark-rigged, she was the best all-round windjammer to date, and the surviving and recently built tall ships of this century are her descendants.

The bustling shipyards of Maine were building the vast majority of these barks. Therefore, the medium clippers were known as down-easters and had been sliding down the ways of that rocky coast well before the Civil War. Trees filled Maine's back yard, and it seemed senseless to build a ship of any other sort of material. Europe's woodlands had long been stripped of its husky timber. At first, iron seemed an unlikely substitute. But when it was rolled into flat plates, a hull made of such a skin was actually only three quarters the weight of the same-sized wooden ship. Ten years later, steel replaced the iron plates and was fifteen percent lighter in the bargain. Medium clippers could now hold more cargo and better withstand the stresses of transatlantic buffeting. The time-honored wooden hull was downgraded. The last such, the "Aryan," was launched from a Maine shipyard in 1893.

LARGE AMERICAN MEDIUM CLIPPER "QUEEN OF CLIPPERS"~ EAST BOSTON, 1853.
(FROM FRENCH PRINT AT SMITHSONIAN, WASHINGTON)

The steel hull had another advantage, for it could be built to unbelievable lengths and widths while maintaining great strength. Wood was too flexible and would give in a larger sized vessel. Soon, steel-hulled medium clippers were reaching the 3000-ton mark. When bark-rigged, she was considered the best all-around sailer ever built ~ and remains so today.

GREAT HULLED SAILERS 1880~1914

Other than the steamship, the medium clipper had an unforeseen enemy ~ rising operating costs. Those square sails required a large crew, and wages meant

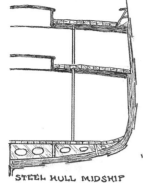

STEEL HULL MIDSHIP
SECTION ~ HALF VIEW.

less profit for the owner. Out of Maine in the 1880s skimmed a new and different answer to greater bankrolls under sail~the great schooner. The amidship sides of the medium clipper were lengthened into a long, straight wooden hull. Over the next twenty years they sprouted four, five and then six "posters," all clothed in only fore~and~aft sails. Her low profile would win no beauty prizes and she was no tall ship, but she needed only half the crew of a square rigger to bring home a large and profitable cargo from her coastal passages.

Then, in 1902, the "Thomas W. Lawson" wallowed forth. With its gigantic hold that was 35 feet deep, 395 feet long, and 50 feet wide, she resembled a floating bath~tub, handled about as well, and was homely as sin. She was the only seven~masted schooner ever built and needed but sixteen crewmen to handle her fore~and~aft sails. Few wages and a huge payload made the "Lawson" cost efficient in the face of steam competition. Disaster struck on an Atlantic run in 1907, when she turned turtle off the Scillies with the loss of all but two sailors.

MAINE GREAT SCHOONER" JACOB B. HASKELL."

In 1902, there was another first ~ the only five-masted full-rigged ship ever launched. In contrast to the "Lawson," the "Preussen" was as decent appearing as she was large~407 feet long and 53 feet in width. She was the pride of the Laeisz family of Germany, the builders of fine ships since 1839. In spite of her size, she needed only a forty-seven-man crew. Even the efficient "Preussen," like her sister tall ships, faced expensive maintenance and the bottoming out of business after World War I. Within five years, most of the Cape Horn ships had disappeared from the seas. A scatter-ing of square riggers, most along the steel-hulled medium clipper lines, survived the scrap heap to keep the old sailing traditions alive.

GERMAN SHIP "PREUSSEN"~THE ONLY 5 MASTED FULL
RIGGER EVER BUILT. 8000 TONS CARGO.

AUXILIARY SAILERS

Perhaps auxiliary square riggers should be mentioned as the last desperate effort of the sailing ships to survive. Combining an engine with sail must have been a landlubber's idea. It seemed reasonable that propellers could allow the windjammer to sail into the wind instead of tacking. Unfortunately, the wind resistance on the masts and riggings made any real head-way impossible. The convenience gained when coming in to dock instead of using tugboats was outweighed by the propeller drag, lost cargo space to the engine and fuel, and the specialized repairs needed ~ to say nothing of the indignity of having to say "If we can't beat steamships, let's join them!"

HULL PAINT AND DECORATIONS

Like Henry Ford's Model "T," the Baltimore schooners came in a choice of colors as long as it was black. The economy-minded builders avoided any contrasting trim or other embellishments. The packets were black as well, but a wide white stripe, punctuated with black portholes, gave a distinctive touch. The hope was that pirates and hostiles would think that these black squares were gunports as on a man-of-war. The half-scale whaler model at New Bedford, as with so many "spouters," continued this tradition. Some of today's tall ships that show this hull-length band are Venezuela's "Simon Bolivar," Russia's "Kruzenshtern," and Great Britain's "Royalist." Smaller vessels in American waters with black ports are North Carolina's brigantine "Meka II," Baltimore's topsail schooner "Pride of Baltimore," and Newport's topsail sloop "Providence."

1963
ARGENTINE SHIP "LIBERTAD" ~ BRONZE.

1937
PRINCE HENRY
THE NAVIGATOR ON
PORTUGAL'S "SAGRES."

American clippers were entirely black~ and it set off their sleek sharp lines to advantage. Medium clippers found no need for change until the turn of the century. Then there were some that boasted of a dark green hull with a gold stripe, but most square riggers held to the black sides or had them painted white. White enhanced the size of a hull in relation to her masts and spars and was more complimentary to small craft with clean lines rather than the larger sailing ship.

1958
GERMAN
BARK "GORCH FOCK."

Mast color~ a buff tint~ has long been the accepted "stick" color. Deck fittings were commonly white or gray, a boon to any seaman on a dark night. Deck houses were also white and stood out smartly against the oiled wooden deck.

As for figureheads, the Baltimore clipper shunned such extravagance. This was in contrast to the man-of-war frigates of the period that were encrusted with massive carved figures~ and even carved wreaths around some gunports of European origin. If the small commercial sailer carried any sort of bow decoration, it would be a simple billethead. This carving would fit into the stemhead of the bow under the bowsprit.

1971
BRITISH SEA
CADET CORPS
BRIG "ROYALIST."

Packets, with their more luxurious first-class accommodations and finely detailed interior woodwork, continued the figurehead tradition. This was much to superstitious Jack Tar's liking, for these wooden-stem lookouts, always searching the horizon with their carved eyes, seemed the very soul and spirit of the ship. They were often in the classical revival style of the early nineteenth century. There was no lack of Greek or Roman gods. Hercules, a popular subject, would have his multiple muscles clothed in a lion's skin. Famous people, such as William Rush's excellent 1815 carving of Ben Franklin, kept his watchful eye on the progress of the ship. Or perhaps a well-known statesman or the ship's owner himself might be so immortalized,

1830-80
BILLET HEADS.

SCROLLHEAD TURNS OUTWARD.   FIDDLEHEAD TURNS UPWARD.

c1815

BEN FRANKLIN BUST
BY WILLIAM RUSH.

probably clothed in classical garments to give that touch of dignity and agelessness.

The clipper ship and their successors, the moderate clippers, carried figureheads that were home-grown American folk art. Each symbolized the ship's name. An Indian chief in full headdress graced the "Red Jacket." A female angel blew her trumpet to make way for the "Flying Cloud." An enormous eagle jutted from the largest wooden clipper ever built, the "Great Republic." A chocolate-brown horned devil was appropriate for the "Styx." The "Champion of the Seas," another of Donald McKay's clippers, carried a full figure of a sailor wearing a checkered shirt, black kerchief, blue jacket, bell-bottomed pants with a black belt and large buckle, and black shoes. This striking figure waved a welcome with his tarpaulin hat. Builder McKay's namesake* clipper was crowned with a highlander wearing the family tartan.

1853

EAGLE
FIGUREHEAD OF THE "GREAT
REPUBLIC" (LIBRARY, STONINGTON, CONNECTICUT)

Of all the figureheads, probably none were more appriciated by the old salts than those of women. Many ships were named after the owner's daughter or wife and carried her likeness. The "Nightingale" honored Jenny Lind, the famous Swedish singer of the 1860s. Generally the carvings emphasized her curves and dress. The fabric billowed aft as though caught by the breeze, and blended into the graceful streamlining of the hull. There were exceptions, for a Captain Rossiter insisted that the backward flow of his figurehead's gown should hang downward instead of making it appear that his clipper was always beating into a headwind.

She would perch on a leaf-and-scroll billethead to give a forward thrust, giving a feeling of motion and life to the wooden lady. So much so, in fact, that legend has it that one seaman would lower himself onto the bobstay and stare up at the curvaceous creature. In his jealousy, he imagined her looking out over the horizon for another lover.

The sailor preferred his women~ship decoration or ashore-to be robust and buxom. Forget subtle colors. They should be primary and gaudy with bright yellow hair, red splotches for cheeks, and a dress of sky blue or green. The sailor was usually a man of simple tastes, and he liked his visions of painted ladies ashore to be reinforced by the figurehead at sea.

Figureheads were carved from a single tree trunk or several large doweled slabs, slanted at the base to fit under the bow. To appear lifelike against the largeness of the ship, the figure was carved three to five inches taller than normal. On a huge ship, however, the figure might be as tall as eight feet and a width of three feet to be in proportion. Busts were usual on smaller sailers.

Pine was favored for its great diameter, ease of carving, and lightness. However, the sea spray was destructive to softer woods, so several figureheads might ornament the bow over the ship's lifetime. Arms were carved within the thickness of the log, close to the body to prevent fracture. Some of the more spectacular carvings had detachable arms. After leaving port, they were removed to prevent damage from those inevitable storms over the horizon.

1847

FIGUREHEAD FROM "CREOLE".
(NATIONAL GALLERY OF ART)

*"DONALD MCKAY."

WIND POWER

Just as a ship was known by her hull, the canvas carried aloft was equally distinctive. Square sails and fore-and-aft sails could be combined in a variety of ways that complemented the design and function of the hull.

Ship   Bark   Barkentine

Full-rigged Brig   Hermaphrodite Brig (Brigantine)   Top-sail Schooner

(FROM THE SEAMAN'S FRIEND, RICHARD HENRY DANA, BOSTON, 1841)

SAIL RIGS ~ The square sails' great spread before the wind was combined with the fore-and-aft sails' ability to point closer into the wind.

SHIP = Three or more masts, all square-rigged and the only true tall ship.

BARK (BARQUE) = Three or more masts, square-rigged except for fore-and-aft-rigged aftermast. The best all-around twentieth-century steel-hulled sailer.

BARKENTINE = Three or more masts, the foremast being square-rigged and the other masts fore-and-aft rig.

BRIG = Two masts, square-rigged with a spanker sail aft of the mizzenmast.

HERMAPHRODITE BRIG = Two masts with a square-rigged foremast, and fore-and-aft mainsail.

TOPSAIL SCHOONER = Two or more masts, fore-and-aft-rigged, with two or more square foremast topsails.

FORE-AND-AFT SCHOONER = Two or more masts, all fore-and-aft-rigged.

Fore & aft Schooner

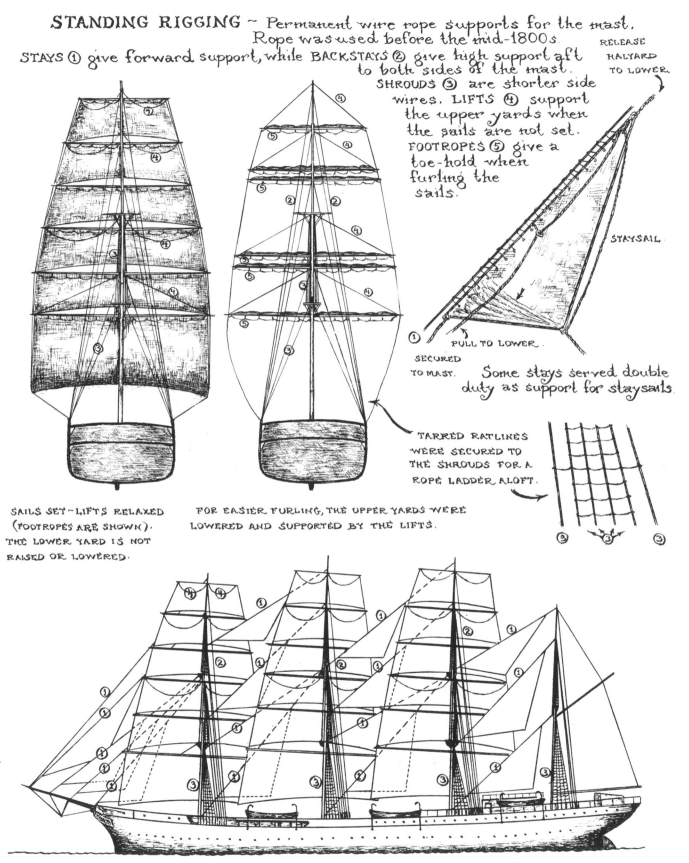

STANDING RIGGING ~ Permanent wire rope supports for the mast. Rope was used before the mid-1800s.
STAYS ① give forward support, while BACKSTAYS ② give high support aft to both sides of the mast.
SHROUDS ③ are shorter side wires. LIFTS ④ support the upper yards when the sails are not set.
FOOTROPES ⑤ give a toe-hold when furling the sails.

RELEASE HALYARD TO LOWER.

STAYSAIL.

① PULL TO LOWER.

SECURED TO MAST. Some stays served double duty as support for staysails.

SAILS SET ~ LIFTS RELAXED (FOOTROPES ARE SHOWN). THE LOWER YARD IS NOT RAISED OR LOWERED.

FOR EASIER FURLING, THE UPPER YARDS WERE LOWERED AND SUPPORTED BY THE LIFTS.

TARRED RATLINES WERE SECURED TO THE SHROUDS FOR A ROPE LADDER ALOFT.

STANDING RIGGING OF A MODERN STEEL-HULLED BARK, THE "NIPPON MARU."

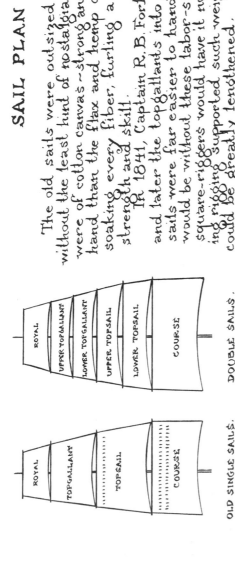

SAIL PLAN

The old sails were outsized and weighty as any shellback would recall without the least kind of nostalgia. In the days of the Yankee clipper, they were of cotton canvas – strong and durable. But they were more difficult to hand than the flax and hemp of Europe. On a cold, gusty night with rain soaking every fiber, furling a sail was a challenge to any seaman's strength and skill.

In 1841, Captain R.B. Forbes split the old-fashioned single topsails and later the topgallants into upper and lower sails. These wide, shallow sails were far easier to handle, and no medium clipper of the 1880's would be without these labor-savers. Our steel-hulled twentieth-century square-riggers would have it no other way. Steel masts and steel wire standing rigging supported such weight that these split sails and their yards could be greatly lengthened.

In earlier days, the topsails were the upper-most sails. The Pilgrims' Mayflower is such an example.

Bands of reef-points, previously used to shorten the huge old sails, had disappeared by the 1880's. Gone, too, were the clipper's skysail and moonrakers that once perched above the royals.

OLD SINGLE SAILS.

ROYAL
TOPGALLANT
TOPSAIL
COURSE

DOUBLE SAILS.

ROYAL
UPPER TOPGALLANT
LOWER TOPGALLANT
UPPER TOPSAIL
LOWER TOPSAIL
COURSE

GAFF TOPSAIL
SPANKER
MIZZEN ROYAL
MIZZEN UPPER TOPGALLANT
MIZZEN LOWER TOPGALLANT
MIZZEN UPPER TOPSAIL
MIZZEN LOWER TOPSAIL
CROSSJACK
MAIN ROYAL
MAIN UPPER TOPGALLANT
MAIN LOWER TOPGALLANT
MAIN UPPER TOPSAIL
MAIN LOWER TOPSAIL
MAINSAIL
FORE ROYAL
FORE UPPER TOPGALLANT
FORE LOWER TOPGALLANT
FORE UPPER TOPSAIL
FORE LOWER TOPSAIL
FORESAIL
FLYING JIB
OUTER JIB
INNER JIB
STAYSAIL

RUNNING RIGGING

"Know the ropes" was no idle phrase on the square-rigger. Real seamanship began at the deck end of these movable ropes. When handled smartly, the sails were set, furled, and trimmed to the angle of the wind. Team effort aboard was a vital part of managing the running rigging.

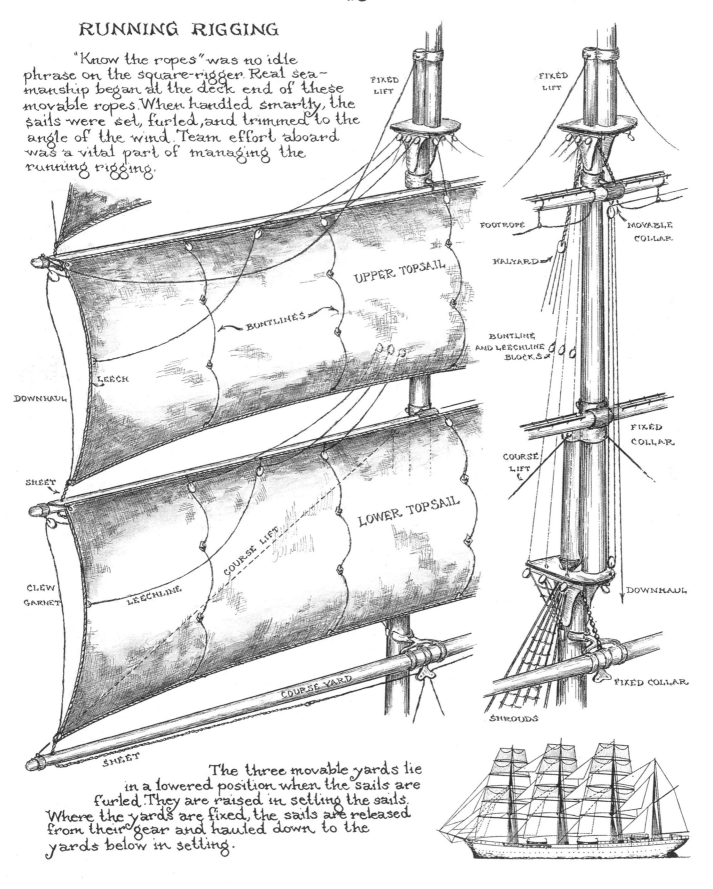

The three movable yards lie in a lowered position when the sails are furled. They are raised in setting the sails. Where the yards are fixed, the sails are released from their gear and hauled down to the yards below in setting.

SETTING SAILS

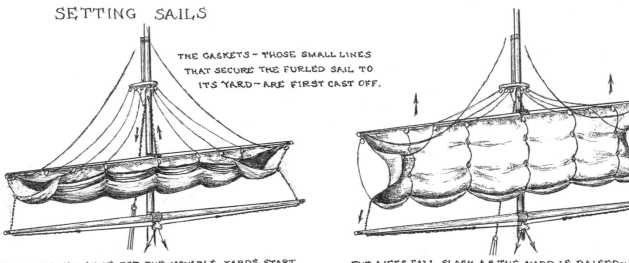

THE GASKETS ~ THOSE SMALL LINES THAT SECURE THE FURLED SAIL TO ITS YARD ~ ARE FIRST CAST OFF.

WHEN THE SAILS ARE SET, THE MOVABLE YARDS START OUT IN THE LOWERED POSITION. THE SHEETS ~ USUALLY CHAIN ~ DRAW THE LOWER CORNERS OF THE SAIL OUT TO THE ENDS OF THE YARD BELOW AS THE SAIL'S YARD IS RAISED.

THE LIFTS FALL SLACK AS THE YARD IS RAISED ~ BEHIND THE YARD, NOT IN FRONT OF IT AS SHOWN IN THE DRAWING. THE LEECHLINES AND BUNTLINES ARE GIVEN SUFFICIENT SLACK SO THAT THEY WILL NOT PREVENT THE SALES FROM SPREADING.

FURLING

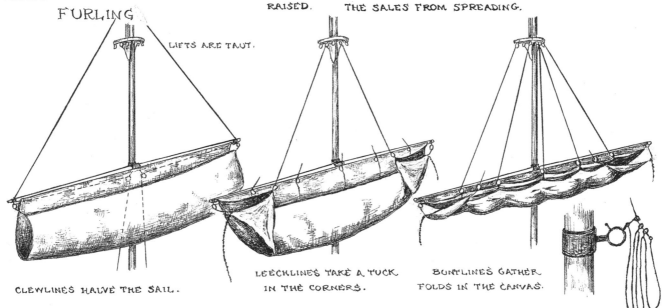

LIFTS ARE TAUT.

CLEWLINES HALVE THE SAIL.

LEECHLINES TAKE A TUCK IN THE CORNERS.

BUNTLINES GATHER FOLDS IN THE CANVAS.

When furling, the movable yards are again lowered as the halyard and sheets are slackened. Clewlines, leechlines and buntlines are hauled in, folding the sail into a manageable form before securing it to the jackstays.

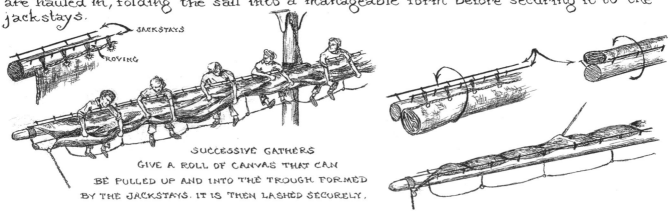

JACKSTAYS

ROVING

SUCCESSIVE GATHERS GIVE A ROLL OF CANVAS THAT CAN BE PULLED UP AND INTO THE TROUGH FORMED BY THE JACKSTAYS. IT IS THEN LASHED SECURELY.

BRACING THE YARDS

Once the sails were set, the yards must be pivoted in the horozontal plane to take advantage of the windpower. Braces were part of the running rigging, and at least a dozen seamen were needed to brace a yard against the force of a high wind. It could be a dangerous business.

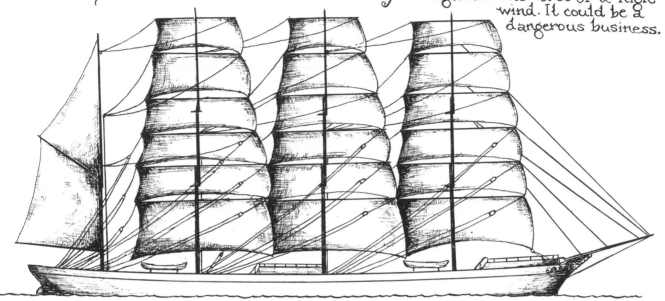

BRACES ON A MODERN STEEL-HULLED BARK.

British Captain J.C.B. Jarvis, a turn-of-the-century idea man who had made many running rigging improvements, came up with a blister-beater known as a brace-winch. Turning a sail required loosening one brace and hauling in on its opposite. By securing one brace to a cone-shaped barrel and the other to a similar reversed cone, a yard brace could be shortened while the other was lengthened a like amount. Three pairs of these winch barrels could turn the most difficult yards to manage — the course, the lower and the upper topsail. Only two very grateful sailors were needed to hand-crank the sails into position.

THE JARVIS BRACE-WINCH.

On today's training ships there is no lack of willing muscle. Generally, the braces are hauled in or loosened by hand as in the pre-Jarvis days. Yet, after a few changes in the ship's course, no cadet could fail to appreciate the impact of the brace-winch and what it meant to a small crew aboard a merchantman.

"BELAY" means to secure a line. The free end of most running rigging, including the braces, was secured around belaying pins along the pinrails and fiferails. Each line (with the exception of the halyards, downhauls, and those to the spanker and gaff topsail) had its mate on a directly opposite belaying pin. As a general rule, the higher the sail, the farther aft would its line be secured on the pinrails. The fiferail, that "U" shaped

BRACE

FIFERAIL

PINRAIL

BRACE

BRACING THE YARDS.

railing at the foot of the mast, held much of the rigging that ran down aft of the mast itself. This orderly and logical placement of each pair of lines must be known by the greenest cadet, or soon enough there might be tons of canvas and spars down around their ears.

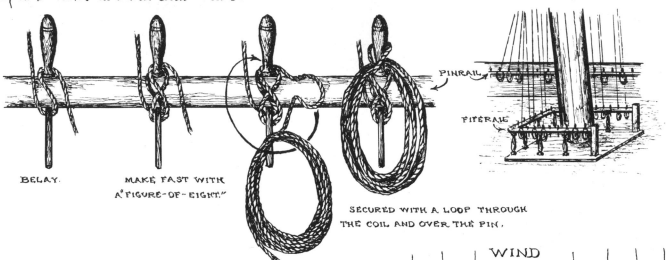

BELAY.

MAKE FAST WITH A "FIGURE-OF-EIGHT."

SECURED WITH A LOOP THROUGH THE COIL AND OVER THE PIN.

PINRAIL

FIFERAIL

UNDERWAY

Rarely did the wind cooperate to blow in the same direction as the ship's course. The dullest hand would have few problems at the steering wheel with the breeze at his back. But sailing into the wind was not only a fact of life at sea ~ it was also something of a puzzle for even the crustiest of shellbacks. Until 1915, that is, when the Massachusetts Institute of Technology first made wind-tunnel tests on sail. The same forces that lifted the wing of an airplane were at work on the acres of canvas. Air flowing against an angled sail is curved out of its path and therefore must speed up before joining the main air current. This creates a greater pressure on the canvas than that passing across the bow. The ship is now moving under this difference of wind pressure.

WIND

POINTS OF SAILING ~ There are three main points of sailing that depend on the heading of the ship and the direction of the wind. Of these, the speed is greatest halfway between running and reaching. Trying to sail closer than 45 degrees into the wind will leave the ship dead in the water.

1. RUNNING ~ WIND DEAD ASTERN.

2. REACHING ~ WIND IS ON THE BEAM.

3. BEATING ~ SAILING INTO WIND AS MUCH AS POSSIBLE.

45°

WORKING THE SHIP

Since a ship can beat upwind at no less than a 45-degree angle, the course must be periodically changed. TACKING was the most efficient way to zigzag toward one's destination. After sailing as close to the wind with as much speed as possible, the bow was swung across the wind to start a new tack.

Certainly the bracing of the yards required quick wits and husky hauling as the ship came about. If not properly and promptly angled, the sails would act as huge brakes as she turned into the wind. Less obvious was the help from the spanker and rudder to kick the stern downwind. Meanwhile, the bow jibs were eased off to spill wind. Once the eye of the wind was crossed, they were trimmed to give a push to the bow as it turned.

TACKING

WIND

The square-rigger might also come about by turning downwind and presenting her stern to the wind rather than her bow. Known as WEARING, it was little used unless light winds gave too little speed for tacking or in heavy winds that might take the sails aback and carry away the masts. Wearing a ship took twice as long as tacking and lost distance by turning away from windward and her destination.

BOXHAULING combined tacking and wearing in a confined body of water such as a harbor or working up a river.

PREDICTING THE WIND'S DIRECTION

Wetting one's finger to tell the direction of the wind had little to recommend it aboard the ocean-going square-riggers. A cruise to distant continents demanded a basic knowledge of how and why the wind blows as it does. Then the captain could predict when the trade winds would speed his ship on its way, or how long he might be going nowhere in those frustrating belts of calms - the doldrums.

Hot air expands and rises. Balloonists fire up the air within the balloon if they expect to be lifted off the ground. When this air cools, the balloonist will return to earth. In like fashion, the heat of the equator sends its hot air aloft to produce high level currents that expand north and south from its belt around the earth. As these atmospheric winds approach the chilly poles, they cool and become surface winds - and our means of getting about by sail. Cool, yet warmer than the polar caps, they rise over the earth's poles. As they approach the heat of the equator, their relative coolness brings them to the sea's surface as the trade winds.

The belts of calms are a result of the cooling atmospheric winds changing places with the warming surface winds. They effectively cancel each other out to create a dead calm - and rain in plenty. The surface winds, after picking up the sea's moisture, dump their cargo on these calm belts. Remaining motionless for days while the skies drench all hands was not one of the voyage's high points.

If the earth had no rotation, these winds would be constant in their south to north or their north to south directions. But since the earth turns from west to east, the winds are altered to blow from the northeast above the equator and southeast below it. These are the trade winds, and are bordered by the calms - the horse latitudes. Always predictable, they blow from the latitudes of 30 degrees north or 30 degrees south in the direction of the equator.

The prevailing winds north of the Calms of Cancer or south of the Calms of Capricorn are more in the north or south polar direction. There, the surface rotation of the earth is much less rapid than that of the greater equatorial circumference.

WINDS AROUND THE WORLD

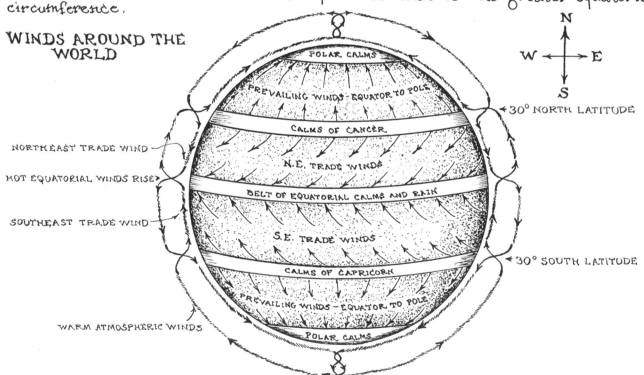

PREVAILING WESTERLY WINDS, TRADE WINDS, AND CALMS AROUND THE WORLD

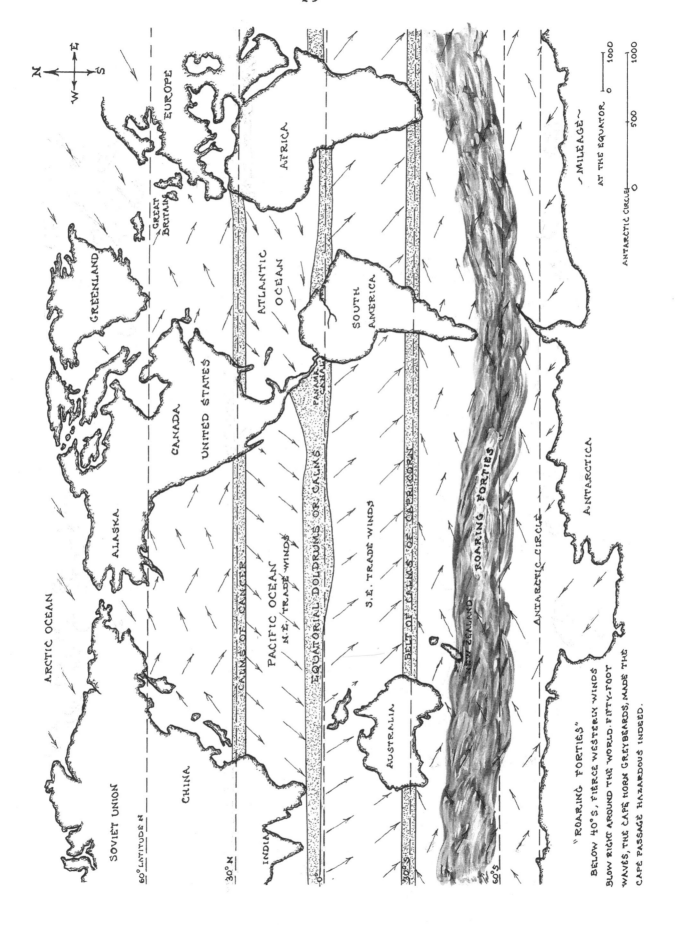

"ROARING FORTIES"

BELOW 40'S, FIERCE WESTERLY WINDS
BLOW RIGHT AROUND THE WORLD. FIFTY-FOOT
WAVES, THE CAPE HORN GREYBEARDS, MADE THE
CAPE PASSAGE HAZARDOUS INDEED.

CARGOES AND PROFITS

That sharp little racer, the Baltimore clipper, had sacrificed cargo space for speed. Because of this she fell into bad company. The War of 1812 was hardly over when Cuban and Spanish captains, under the guise of legitimate merchants, began buying the clippers from the small shipyards that peppered the Delaware and Chesapeake Bays. Then it was off to Cuba, the first leg of a slaving expedition to the west coast of Africa. Once the hold was packed with the unfortunates, body to body, they were hurried off to some uninhabited shores in Cuban waters.

The key to successful slaving was speed. A slow passage could mean a greater number of deaths and a proportionally lower profit. And the British navy was prowling the African coast and the westerly sea lanes. Both they and the United States had outlawed slave trading in 1807, and the King's ships were making the Cuban run very chancy indeed. Any sort of armament was so much extra baggage against naval firepower, and out-running the heavier frigates kept the slavers in business. The British successfully countered with clipper-style vessels of their own.

When capture was a certainty, the slavers' black cargo would be jettisoned overboard to destroy the evidence. Often, for the same reason, the little clippers would be torched at a Cuban anchorage. It seemed better to lose a relatively inexpensive craft than to be rounded up ashore by a landing party.

CHARLESTON NEWSPAPER, 1766, BEFORE THE SLAVE TRADE BECAME ILLEGAL.

From Cuba, the kidnapped blacks were smuggled in small groups to southern mainland plantations or a South American port where slavery was still legal. America's Revenue patrols, with their own extreme Baltimore clippers re-rigged as brigs and brigantines, did a creditable job intercepting these deliveries. But until the Civil War put an end to the politics of human bondage, our Navy's efforts lacked much of the idealism and bulldog determination that was seen under British sail.

1791 PRINT OF SLAVE STOWAGE ON THE "BROOKES" OUT OF LIVERPOOL. UPPER ILLUSTRATION SHOWS THE 6-FOOT-WIDE PLATFORM THAT WAS RAISED ABOVE THE DECK. C=MEN, G=WOMEN E=BOYS.
(FROM CLARKSON'S "ABSTRACT OF THE EVIDENCE," 1791)

SEAL OF THE COMMITTEE FOR ABOLITION OF THE SLAVE TRADE, FORMED IN 1787.

Slavers were not the only specialists in atrocities for hard cash. When the War of 1812 ended, merchant ships were free to go about their business as usual. The Caribbean was a very large exception, for nests of pirates had multiplied along the Cuban shoreline, its surrounding islands, and Florida as well. Any small unarmed vessel was fair game for their swift clippers. In the old Bluebeard tradition, these cut-throats would swarm aboard, rape and pillage, and frequently murder the crew to a man. They were firm believers in the old saying "Dead cats don't mew."

19TH-CENTURY "JOLLY ROGER" ENSIGN FLOWN FROM THE MIZZEN-PEAK.

By 1820, the world's news-papers were screaming headlines that seemed hard to believe.

One such, in 1824, was said to stir up such indignation among the American citizenry that the Navy redoubled its efforts to clear the West Indies of the last remnants of such sea scum.

It seemed that the Maine brig "Betsey" had struck a rock off one of Cuba's keys. Their lifeboats were attacked by Spaniards who bound the crew, hauled them ashore and told them that "Americans were very good beef for their knives." Captain

PIRATICAL BARBARITY.

BROADSIDE- "THE HORRID MASSACRE OF THE UNFORTUNATE CREW OF THE SLOOP 'ELIZA ANN' BY PIRATES, MARCH, 1825." (COLLECTION OF F.B.C. BRADLEE.)

Hilton was promptly beheaded, and the executions that followed were too shocking to be described by the press. Second Mate Daniel Collins received a glancing knife blow that fortunately cut his bonds. Although severely wounded, he managed to escape into the mangroves. There he slept at night, resting his weariness enough to swim from key to key by daylight. Somehow he survived hunger, thirst, intense heat, and mosquitoes to reach Cuban authorities and tell his story.

Certainly the United States hadn't idled away time until the "Betsey" outrage. Between 1820 and 1825, British and American naval forces were cooperating to ferret out and destroy the pirate strongholds. Extreme Baltimore clippers, well manned by the Revenue Marine Service, were particularly effective running down the enemy at sea. In 1820, Congress authorized the "Mosquito Fleet," so named because some of the craft were of small size and draft to enter the shallow harbors and bays throughout the West Indies. By 1825, the pirate menace had passed into history.

It might be mentioned that the British had a no-nonsense approach for those they captured. A pirate dangling from a stretch of rope was

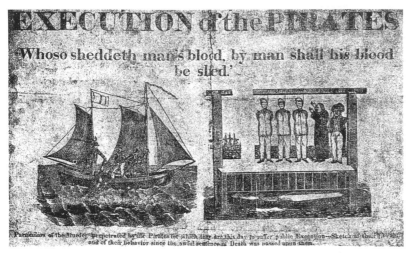

BROADSIDE CONCERNING A SPANISH SCHOONER TAKEN BY PIRATES IN 1818. THE PIRATES WERE EXECUTED AT SCITUATE HARBOR, MASSACHUSETTS. (COLLECTION OF F.B.C. BRADLEE.)

likely to cause few problems. Since the Americans were supposed to ship their catches back to the States for trial, it was not uncommon for the officers to turn them over to the King's ships for a speedier solution.

The little clipper had other outlaw admirers. The opium trade route from India to China made many a pocket jingle ~ and these swift vessels were in demand. British traders were enthusiasts of these dark dealings ~ until Hong Kong passed an "Ordinance Against Piracy" in the 1850s. With their usual efficiency, the British Navy then swept the length of China's coast free of the smuggling operations.

Lest she be misjudged, the Baltimore clipper saw service in many honorable pursuits. An ex-privateer from the 1812 conflict, the schooner "Chasseur," was changed to the brigantine rig and set speed records on the China trade routes. Small specialized and perishable cargoes such as coffee from Brazil or fruits from the West Indies made this little vessel a real commercial asset.

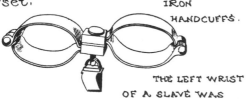

IRON HANDCUFFS. THE LEFT WRIST OF A SLAVE WAS PADLOCKED TO THE RIGHT OF ANOTHER.

OPIUM SMOKERS IN NEW YORK CONTINUED THEIR HOMELAND HABIT. (WINSLOW HOMER ~ HARPER'S WEEKLY, MARCH 7, 1874.)

ABOARD THE PACKET

The sturdy packets were ready and willing to carry anything and anyone anywhere for a price. As for the passengers, that price could buy relative comfort of the first-class cabins or quite the opposite in the second-class and steerage sections. One of the former, Charles Dickens, wrote from New York in 1842, "Below here by the waterside, where the bowsprits stretch across the footway and almost thrust themselves into the windows, lie the noble American vessels which have made their packet service the finest in the world." This was unexpected praise from one of our severest critics. But the English novelist was well aware of his own country's packet shortcomings, and that was the truth of it.

This was the period when the qualities of the sharp Baltimore clipper and the all-purpose packet were combined by American shipbuilders to produce the classic clipper packet. Extremely fast, elegant with clean streamlining, yet roomy and airy, she made the transatlantic passage almost a pleasure. It was not always so, for the old packets from 1820 and several decades thereafter were small, bulky, and cramped for space. Sometimes the builder, agent, and captain each owned an eighth of the ship, while the owner claimed the remainder. It was to their advantage to schedule frequent sailings, cram the hold, and push the canvas.

The packets were ready for the mass exodus from Europe when our anti-emigration laws were repealed in 1825. The 1830 revolt in Poland, the enormous crop failure of 1846 in Germany and Holland, and the 1846-47 Irish potato famine filled the packets to overflowing. By the end of the nineteenth century, millions more had become United States citizens— Scandinavians heading for the northwest lumbering industry, Chinese, Russians, Austrians, and Greeks among them.

These hardy, determined, and often poverty-stricken souls needed all the stamina and optimism they could muster. Liverpool was the usual port of embarkation~ a dark hole of a place that specialized in con men (otherwise known as emigration agents), rat-infested boarding houses while awaiting departure, bands of thieves, and even stories of baggage held for ransom.

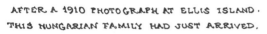

AFTER A 1910 PHOTOGRAPH AT ELLIS ISLAND.
THIS HUNGARIAN FAMILY HAD JUST ARRIVED.

Those fortunate enough to find themselves aboard the earlier packets faced a special kind of hell. As owners cashed in on this human bonanza, old and rotten ships were pressed into service, jammed with passengers and cargo until the old timbers were ready to burst. Some did. These were the "coffin ships." Overloaded and unseaworthy, many were lost at sea. Between 1847 and 1853, for example, fifty-nine emigrant ships were lost with all aboard.

Thanks to crusader Samuel Plimsoll, the British passed a law requiring all vessels to have safe load markings.

A foot-long white line, painted amidships, took the guesswork out of knowing when the ship was fully loaded~and no more. She would be "down to her marks."

THE PLIMSOLL LINE*

Before this and other safety measures, the average emigrant found himself shoe-horned into that dark and stifling fore section of the ship known as the steerage. Racks of bunks were added by the ship's carpenter just before sailing to ensure that all bodies were closely packed. A place to sleep and use of a common stove were the only comforts provided. False passenger lists were common, as with the Irish emigrant packet that sailed in 1847 with thirty-two listed berths but with two hundred and seventy-three persons actually aboard.

Early on, everyone in steerage supplied their own food and cooking utensils. Then English and

"GIVE ME YOUR TIRED, YOUR POOR, YOUR HUDDLED MASSES YEARNING TO BREATHE FREE..." THIS IMPRESSIVE SYMBOL HAS RAISED HER TORCH OF LIBERTY TO ALL NEWCOMERS SINCE 1886.

* THE CIRCLE AROUND THE LOAD LINE INDICATED THE MIDDLE OF THE SHIP.

American legislation required that food rations be provided. Three quarts of water were issued daily. Each week, second cabin and steerage passengers were doled up two ounces of tea, eight of sugar, nine of molasses, one pound of wheat flour, two-and-a-half pounds of navy bread, four pounds of oatmeal, two of rice, one of salt pork, and any vinegar necessary.

Sanitation was a low packet priority. Often the lavatory was as near as the side of the ship. To compound the problem, passengers were allowed above deck only if the weather was decent. Under such primitive living conditions, it was not surprising that the emigrants were easy marks for typhoid, typhus, cholera, and small pox.

EXAMINATION OF STEERAGE PASSENGERS, 1887. A HOSPITAL SHIP IS ANCHORED IN THE DISTANCE. (HARPER'S WEEKLY, OCTOBER 1887)

These were the adventurous and hardy spirits who would soon join the great American melting pot as new citizens.

The emigrant trade was part of the "Triangular Run" and so heavily traveled that one would almost expect grooves to be worn in the sea lanes. From Liverpool

CARGO HOLD OF THE NEW YORK~ LIVERPOOL PACKET "CORNELIUS GRINNELL," LAUNCHED IN 1850.
(PAINTING BY HARRY SAUNDERS, IN THE McKAY COLLECTION.)

to New York or Boston it was human cargo. The next leg of the voyage headed for Savannah or Mobile to be loaded with cotton, ready for the return trip to Liverpool. The "Jenny Lind" slid down the ways in 1848; she was the first of the cotton-carrying "kettle bottoms." She was craftily designed with a swell in the hull below the waterline. Since tonnage ~ and taxes ~ were calculated by measuring the width of the deck, the design was prudent for more profit. Into this ballooned-out cavity was packed the open-ended cotton bales, compressed so tightly with a jack that three could be jammed into a space that two would reasonably occupy. So enthusiastic was this practice that more than one deck was known to be lifted off her stanchions!

CARGO WINCH. THE UPPER ROLLER LIFTED OR LOWERED LIGHT CARGO INTO THE HOLD. THE GREATER GEARING POWER OF THE UPPER ROLLER WAS USED FOR HEAVIER LOADS.

THE PARBUCKLE WAS A ROPE SLING THAT WAS HELPFUL FOR ROLLING BARRELS UP AN INCLINED PLANE TO THE DECK.

The great 1830s upsurge in trade sent the packets around treacherous Cape Horn. California, although not yet gold conscous, was isolated and in want of as many different goods as one could lay a tongue to. Between 1830 and 1850 Dana's Two Years Before The Mast listed pages of trade merchandise that included blue drill, calico, blue jeans, carpets, thread, bandanas, horn combs, tobacco, sugar, ale, cocoa, almonds, flour, tin boxes of sardines, hoes, iron pots, nails, furniture, rifles, fishing hooks, dishes, white pine boards, Spanish playing cards, and corn brooms!

The return trip often featured "California bank notes" ~ otherwise known as cattle hides. Dana told of curing and loading these hides, some 39,000 of them, along with 31,000 horns (to be softened and pressed into combs, handles, and the like) and about 800 beaver pelts for the London market.

IVORY CLUB USED ON SEALS FOR A RETURN CARGO. FROM THE EARLIEST DAYS OF THE NINETEENTH CENTURY TO 1850, THE WEST COAST OF SOUTH AMERICA, PACIFIC NORTHWEST, AND THE ANTARCTIC YIELDED SKINS UNTIL THE SEALS NEARED EXTINCTION. (MYSTIC SEAPORT, CT.)

THE GOLDEN ERA OF WHALING PEAKED BETWEEN 1825 AND 1860. THE ROOMY BARK-RIGGED PACKETS MADE MANY A FORTUNE AND SOCIAL PRESTIGE FOR THE OWNERS.

These were the days when speed and enterprise could make a handsome profit. As early as 1833, New England was turning her frozen ponds into hard cash by rushing slabs of ice packed in sawdust to the West Indies. These ice ships, or "freezers," initially had trouble convincing crews that their cargo wouldn't melt and leave them awash. There was also resistance from the insurance companies, for wet sawdust became inflammable, and a ship on fire was a poor risk indeed. One clever Yankee made a handsome profit by freezing fresh apples in the ice cakes, giving the islanders a taste of fruit unlike their own. The skipper might return to home port with kegs of molasses, much of which was destined to become American rum.

MOVING OUT THE ICE.

CLIPPER CARGO

When that smelly, smoke-belching oddity, the steamship, first took to the water, few took her very seriously. Not for long hauls, at any rate. But then the stubby steamer "Sirius" huffed and puffed her

The Cork Steam-Ship Company's
STEAM SHIP
SIRIUS

way across the Atlantic, taking just eighteen days and ten hours from Cork to New York. Surface condensers made the run possible on fresh water, with no need for the damaging sea water in the boilers. Still, her clanking innards and fuel storage took much too much space for extensive cargo trade~say, around Cape Horn.

By 1845, a new and sharply styled beauty was ready to take on the challenge of steam, be it the far East or whatever. She was John W. Griffiths' "Rainbow," square~ rigged to the skies

BLACK
LEATHER VALISE USED
BY CAPTAIN RUFUS SOULÉ RANDALL TO
HOLD HIS SHIP'S PAYROLL.
(MAINE MARITIME MUSEUM, BATH)

and just the answer to America's mania for speed. Although she was 750 tons, her sleek hull had sacrificed some of the cargo space of the packets~to the concern of no one. She was a specialist in small and valuable goods at premium rates of $1.40 per cubic foot.

Witness the success of the "Sovereign of the Seas." In a single passage to San Francisco in 1852, she unloaded a cargo of flour at $44.00 a barrel. Added to the passenger receipts, she cleared a grand total of $98,000 for this single passage. Opportunities were everywhere. The next port of call was Honolulu, where a cargo of whale oil was taken aboard from New England whalers hunting the area. This saved the "spouters" the long trip home, and they could continue cruising. Then back in San Francisco, the "Sovereign" took on a large grizzly bear, a rainbow bear, a wolf, a wild-cat, a coyote, and a leopard for exhibition at the Crystal Palace back in New York!

The first clippers were just in time for the '49 California gold rush. Would-be pros-pectors lined up to pay the tidy sum of $150~$200 a head. When one was heady with gold fever, no amount seemed unreasonable. Whole towns seemed to catch the disease, and many a hopeful would sail with his neighbors with a send-off sermon still ringing in his ears. The favorite text of the minister's message was said to be Genesis 2:12~"...and the gold of that land is good."

One hundred and fifty of these "Greyhounds of the Seas" were built between 1850 and 1853 alone. The clipper appeared to be the ulti-mate answer to any sea-going enterprise. With the repeal of the British Navigation acts~the

Glidden & Williams' LINE For San-Francisco!
FROM LEWIS WHARF.

The very superior A1 clipper ship

CLIPPER SHIP
California!

HENRY BARBER,
Commander,

Is now in berth with one half her cargo on board. This ship was built expressly for the trade, and is in every way a most desirable conveyance. Her en-gagements are large, and we confidently expect to despatch her at an early day.
Shippers will oblige by forwarding their goods promptly.

FOR FREIGHT......APPLY TO *Glidden & Williams,*
NO. 114 STATE STREET, BOSTON.
Agents in San-Francisco......MESSRS. MEADER, LOLOR & Co.

(BOSTONIAN SOCIETY COLLECTION)

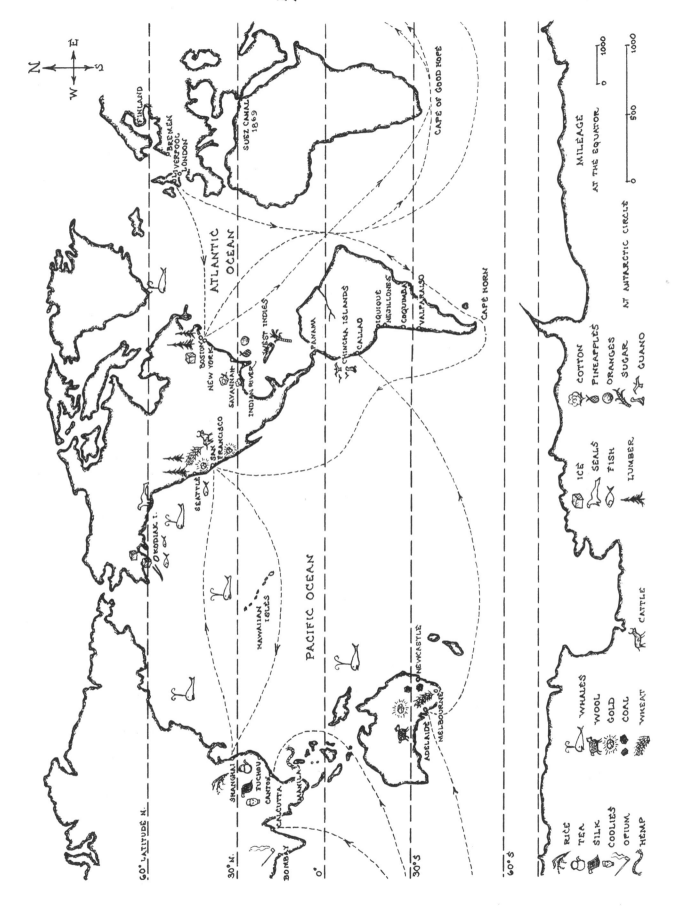

NINETEENTH~CENTURY TRADE ROUTES AND CARGOES UNDER SAIL.

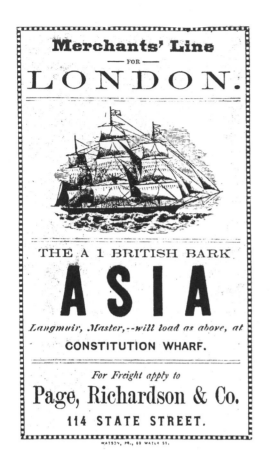

(BOSTONIAN SOCIETY COLLECTION)

same year gold was discovered ~ trade was no longer limited to British shipping. The run from California to China was now well worthwhile. Tea could be Bought in the Orient at five pence a pound, and unloaded on the English tea-totalers for sixty pence a pound.

Distant Australia entered the world trade market in 1854 with not one but two attractions. Gold was found in quantity there as well, and hordes of Englishmen were in need of a clipper ticket to stake their claim to fortune. Further, native sheep had been crossed with an Indian breed to produce a high-quality wool. London was ready and willing to pay forty-three pence a pound that cost the shipper four-and-a-half pence. There were several drawbacks. Wool was combustible and a real concern. Also, unwanted passengers ~ fleas ~ came aboard with the bales, and hungry clouds of the critters frequently drove the crew topside.

Then, after a short twenty years, the extreme clipper was suddenly a graceful has-been ~ a ship without a purpose. The 1857 railway across the Isthmus of Panama, with steamer connections at both ends, short-circuited the clippers' lengthy Cape Horn passage. The Civil War was not far behind, and trade on the high seas had little consideration when the survival of the Union was at stake. There was still a place for specialized trade in China tea and Australian wool. Small ~ rarely over 1200 tons ~ yacht-like clippers from English ports soon had these sea lanes to themselves ~ and well in hand. With deeper hulls, narrow beams, and sharp clipper lines, they were wet ships but well suited for fast passages or ghosting along when wind failed. A prime example of these tea and wool clippers is the "Cutty Sark," now restored and awaits the visitor at London.

Meanwhile, the "Down-Easters" ~ the American medium clippers ~ had been doing a lively general trade business with wheat from California, rice from India, hemp from Manila, tea and coolies

BRITISH TEA CLIPPER SHIP "CUTTY SARK," BUILT IN 1869.

from China, sugar from the Hawaiian Isles, lumber and tinned salmon from the Pacific northwest, and coffee, hides, and other products from Chile and Peru. "Other products" included guano ~ a Peruvian word for manure. These nitrates were in demand as fertilizer for enriching the farmlands of England and Holland and along the United States' Atlantic coastline. The short, straight midsection of these modified clippers held the assorted cargoes easily.

Through the centuries, the small and lumpy islands off Peru were home for generations of pelicans, penguins, albatross, and cormorants. There they left

ASIA ISLAND, WITH DARK PATCHES WHERE THE GUANO HAD BEEN DUG.
A NORWEGIAN BARK IS LEAVING WITH THE CARGO. (1923 PHOTOGRAPH.)

their mementos ~ droppings that rose to two hundred feet in places. With practically no rainfall along the arid coastline to wash it away, the islands looked like so many cakes with yellow icing.

There, naked Chinese coolies and a scattering of Peruvian criminals worked out their short lives under the broiling sun, breathing in overpowering ammonia fumes in a haze of guano dust. Being soft deposits ~ the consistency of pepper ~ workers sank to their knees in the diggings. It was the worst kind of slavery imaginable.

In 1865 alone, these forsaken souls dug more than 20,000 shiploads of 2000 tons each. Sails were sent down during the loading, for the fumes tended to rot the canvas. If not loaded in bulk, any bags of the powder were likely to be disintegrated by the end of the voyage. Many downgraded extreme clippers, those once-graceful queens of the seas, suffered a final indignity by being sentenced to this trade. Yet demand made this a profitable business, and there was little enough of that in the post-Civil War depression. By the early twentieth century, chemical plants were able to make nitrates in quantity. The islands, considerably tidier, were given back to the birds.

FEWER MARKETS ~ MORE COMPETITION

By the 1880s, these bulk imperishables were helping the sailing ships to survive (only later steamers could refrigerate the more fragile foodstuffs). Maine was sending her four-to six-masted schooners along the American coastline to offer low delivery rates for lumber, coal, lime, granite, and ice. Such cargoes were made to order for these economical fore-and-afters, skillfully managed by their small crews.

Both wooden and steel medium clippers seemed to be holding their own by the turn of the century. There were profits still to be made in Australian wheat, and there was a decent market in general merchandise ~ oil, machinery (including locomotives), pig-iron, wool, cotton, jute, and manufactured goods. Still, steamships continued to multiply and prosper as they competed for the wind ships' trading ports. It must have been a real embarrassment for a windjammer of any description to haul a load of coal to the West Indies or Panama for their arch-enemies to use on local runs.

WALRUS TOOTH PIN FROM ALASKA.

IVORY LETTER OPENER FROM CHINA.

About this time the Laeisz family introduced their "P" Line* of huge steel four-and five-masted square-riggers. German efficiency and precision provided hulls with a capacity of upward to 7000 tons, yet they could be handled by a crew of forty or so sailors. Some were outfitted specifically for the guano trade, and all were of such strength that the hazards of Cape Horn gave little concern. These giants of the high seas were fast enough to give the "coal eaters" a taste of their wake at sixteen knots. They were a handsome example of the shipbuilding art, and a sight to be remembered by the crustiest of old shellback sailors. It seemed that the steamship would at last have her comeuppance.

LOUSE SCRATCHER TRIMMED WITH BLEACHED HUMAN HAIR FROM PORT MORESBY, NEW GUINEA.

* THE FIRST LETTER OF EACH SHIP BEGAN WITH "P".

MANDARIN SHOE –
CHINA.

TEA POT –
JAPAN.

TROPICAL WOOD
JEWEL BOX –
SIAM.

COLLECTED BY CAPTAIN WELLS AND CAPTAIN ALEXANDER
OF HALLOWELL, MAINE. (MAINE MARITIME MUSEUM, BATH)

It was little more than a forecastle pipe dream. Powered vessels had unexpected allies, and not the least was the 1914 opening of the Panama Canal. That tall ship specialty ~ bucking the headwinds of the Cape Horn "Roaring Forties" ~ was suddenly a worthless ability. While the steamers happily chugged through the Atlantic-Pacific shortcut, the big ditch was of no use for those under sail. The Belt of Calms over on the Pacific side left them dead in the water.

Other problems crowded in on the windjammer. Since the "coal eaters" had become the darlings of the seas early in the twentieth century, construction capital was largely funneled in their direction. For the young man who wished to follow the sea, the advantages of steam seemed obvious. Even those apprentices who had trained under sail were likely to opt for a comfortable steamship berth that could offer more pay, few "all hands" calls, and a less-demanding knowledge of the sea in exchange for a rather humdrum existence. The finely honed teamwork that characterized deep-water sailing gradually disintegrated, and many a proud old windship went to Davy Jones because of inexperienced hands or sloppy seamanship.

Full-riggers, with their acres of canvas and miles of rigging, were becoming increasingly expensive to build and maintain. Crews were large and the ports of call distant, all of which translated into a hefty payroll. Insurance costs became burdensome (a fact of life at sea or at home), and there were the usual levies for pilotage, tug towing, port dues, wharfage, and dry docking. Meanwhile, freight charges for those old standbys of timber, coal, and grain tumbled to less than half their previous rates.

The Germans were still competing with the steamship trade until their World War I defeat. The magnificent Laeisz ships were turned over to the victors, who more often than not let them quietly turn to

LUMBER BARROW USED TO LOAD MAINE
SCHOONERS WITH HARDWOOD. 19TH AND
EARLY 20TH CENTURY.

(PEABODY MUSEUM, SALEM.)

rust at dockside. The Laeisz Line bought back some of those that were still in decent condition and fleshed out their fleet with some newly constructed vessels ~ the last commercial sailing ships to be built. They were just in time for the great post-war trade slump that bankrupted sail and steam owners alike. By the beginning of World War II, most of the "P" Liners had retired. Their "Passat," the last commercial tall ship on the high seas, made her last grain voyage in 1956.

Captain Gustav Erikson, a champion of square-rigged sailing, found opportunity knocking following the Kaiser's downfall. From his base in Finland's Åland Islands, he purchased a number of three-and four-masted barks at bargain prices. When a ship outlived its usefulness and was no longer seaworthy, he would sell her off for scrap and replace her with another orphaned windship. With relatively little invested, the Captain felt no need to pay stiff insurance premiums. For a while, Erikson did well enough hustling Australian wheat around the Horn, with perhaps a delivery of coal or timber on the way. He was a frugal, sea-wise owner who made the last days of shipping pay off ~ until the surplus of old windjammers ran out.

NEW CHALLENGES FOR SAIL

UNITED STATES NAVAL CADETS ON A SAIL TRAINING CRUISE.

The tall ship was far more than a means of bringing back a profitable cargo from strange and exotic lands. She was a floating home for countless men who chose to follow the sea. Life under sail had interwoven their lives with salty traditions, superstitions, hard work on dangerous seas, a language that could make sense only to a square-rigger sailor, and a pride in their seamanship abilities that could send them up the ratlines in the face of the worst gale Cape Horn had to offer. Under sail, each was a man among men, depending on his shipmates to work as a team while anticipating nature's fickle ways with wind and wave.

The lore of the sea and the adventures that awaited just beyond the horizon were freely shared over a pipeful or a cup of coffee in the forecastle. Newcomers~youngsters fresh from the comforts of home~listened to and absorbed the yarns of their elders and would some day pass on what they had learned to other deck boys or apprentices. It was neither fitting nor proper that the challenges of the tall ship should sink along with the last of the commercial square-riggers.

SAILOR'S PIPE, SHEATHED IN FINELY WORKED KNOTS.
(WILBUR, PIRATES & PATRIOTS OF THE REVOLUTION - 1973-1984)

Although few could imagine a rebirth after World War II, there were those who urged a new concept of the old deck boy and apprenticeship learning experience. Seasoned instructors would introduce young people to the practicalities of sea life aboard a sailing classroom. The sail training programs caught on and moved ahead. Old square-riggers were salvaged and restored for the purpose. New training vessels, many along the modified clipper lines, continue to move down the ways.

Today, training on the high seas is as varied as the vessels now under canvas. From families shipping out for a day's run to the lengthy cruises under formal merchant marine and naval instruction, the thrill of sailing may be shared by everyone. But all should be forewarned~ sea fever may become contagious!

CADET TRAINING SHIP

STEAMSHIP   LARGE STEEL MEDIUM CLIPPER   MEDIUM CLIPPER   EXTREME CLIPPER   PACKET   BALTIMORE CLIPPER

THE OLD APPRENTICE SYSTEM

Captain Erikson may have cut his costs to the keel, but he never stinted on his enthusiasm for the apprentice system. Over one hundred boys from all over the world, including the United States, were eager to learn practical seamanship under knowledge- able mates. Under Finnish law, it was required that the boys be at least sixteen years of age, present two doctors' certificates stating that "...the work of a seaman will not be harmful to the applicant," a letter from a clergyman that vouched for his character, and of course a letter of parental consent.

Most countries, however, were far less rigid in their screening process. Generally, the boys had only to be

BECKET ON MINIATURE CHEST THAT HELD PAPERS OF SHIP ACUSHNET. HERMAN MELVILLE MADE WHALING VOYAGE TO SOUTH SEAS IN 1837.

(ASHLEY BOOK OF KNOTS, 1944.)

SEA CHEST BELONGING TO IRISH EMIGRANT JAMES MCKIERAN, c.1848.
(MYSTIC SEAPORT, CONNECTICUT)

twelve years old, and their families pay a premium (as with the Erikson fleet) for their sons to gain experience for a berth as future mates and masters. From four to twelve candidates bunked aboard in their own quarters in the maindeck cabin amidships. Sea chests were their only wardrobe, for there were no pegs for hanging clothes. Chests also doubled as seating (rarely used on the busy square-rigger!) and as a washstand for the daily ration of fresh water. Their dress uniforms distinguished them from the what-ever clothing of the forecastle crowd. For example, British apprentices of this century wore double-breasted, brass-buttoned suits. Topping off such splendor were small peaked caps with the badge of the owner's line flag. Tradition has it that the sleeve buttons were to prevent the homesick youngsters from wiping their sniffles there.

The best cure for missing the family was work ~ hard and plenty of it. Apprentices knew no pampering. They did the same chores as did deck boys and ordinary seamen, ate the same food, stood the same watches, and were laid low by the same sea-sickness. It was a practical hands-on seamanship course, and each was expected to do his share of splicing, rigging mats, sennets that protected the ropes from fraying, and all manner of fancy knots. Still, the quality of shipboard learning depended on the master. Most held regular navigation classes aft, but there were other skippers who looked on the candidates as a source of cheap labor and gave little in return.

The apprentice system ended its long history when the commercial square-riggers died out during World War II. It had supplied the owners of merchant vessels with knowledgeable officers ~ but there was a better way. The school-ship concept now brings the skills of sailing to everyone ~ from those wishing a short salty sampling to the owners of small sailers who hope to improve their seamanship under ocean-wise veterans.

THE SCHOOL SHIPS

MERCHANT MARINE ~ Formal schooling aboard square-riggers for training merchant marine officers began well over a century ago in the far-visioned Scandinavian countries. The benefits from building character into their impressionable youth through the challenges of the sea were well appreciated. Skilled teacher-officers assured the success of the first sailing school ship ~ the Swedish brig "Carl Johan" ~ in commission from 1848 to 1878. Other noteworthy training ships followed, such as the full-rigged 1882 "Georg Stage" of Denmark. Renamed the "Joseph Conrad," this historic ship may now be seen at Mystic Seaport in Connecticut. Her 1935 namesake replacement is one of today's outstanding tall ships.

Another of that country's training ships has close ties with the United States. The "Danmark" was vis-iting the 1939 World's Fair at New York when World War II began. She remained here for the duration of the war and was loaned to the United States

THE "JOSEPH CONRAD," ONCE OWNED BY AUTHOR~CAPTAIN ALAN VILLIERS.

Coast Guard. Five thousand of our Coast Guard cadets were trained on the "Danmark" before she returned to her liberated home port. By 1945, the Coast Guard was convinced of the value of sail training and replaced her with the "Eagle" ~ part of Germany's war reparations.

The Scandinavians moved ahead with their merchant marine schools. In 1877, a grass-roots effort by Norwegian citizens and ship owners resulted in the funding of a stationary sail ship for underprivileged boys. She was replaced

BOW OF THE
CHRISTIAN RADICH.

by a graceful high-seas square-rigger in 1915, thanks to the generosity of merchant Christian Radich. Her 1939 successor still carries her benefactor's name. Unfortunately, the German Navy confiscated and then sank her during World War II. After that conflict, she was raised and restored to her original condition by the Christiana Schoolship Association of Oslo.

Other Scandinavian merchant training ships are supported as well by public-spirited citizens without assistance from the state. Their reward lies wholly in the mature, well-rounded officers who serve their shores under sail or steam.

Since the only cargo a training ship carries is young people, there are no profits to plow back into maintenance. In the late nineteenth century, Congress voted to subsidize merchant marine sail training for those states wishing to do so. With those funds, New York established a school in 1875. Other states followed, and Massachusetts and New York still maintain their sea schools under the original act. Recent legislative changes have made possible other maritime academy sail-training schools in Maine, Michigan, California, and Texas. For the most part, these vessels are sloops and ketches.

NAVAL TRAINING~ In 1944, a Philippine Sea typhoon devastated the American fleet. According to Admiral Ernest J. King, U.S.N., the loss in men and ships was the worst that the Navy suffered in all of World War II. The Admiral placed the blame squarely on poor seaman-ship~ a lack of preparedness and appreciation for nature's sudden fury at sea.

SMALLER SAIL-TRAINING VESSELS.

SLOOP.

KETCH.

Today, naval midshipmen throughout the world face a maze of atomic-age technical advances before shipping aboard a nuclear-powered ship. By contrast, their concentrated schooling includes a stint before the mast. There they have intimate contact with the changing winds, tides, and currents. Through a team effort with fellow cadets, each comes to terms with the elements and works with and not against them. There's initiative, alertness, self-confidence, and a real appreciation of the ocean when heavy weather threatens to shred the canvas above them.

The cadets' experience aboard a sail-training vessel under expert instruction provides the basic skills necessary to become good officers. No huge powered ship, smashing its way into a headwind of whitecaps, can provide such lessons. As the saying of their sea-going ancestors goes, "Only those who brave its dangers know the mysteries of the sea."

Until World War II, Germany's naval school ship fleet was the largest around the globe. These and other handsome steel medium clippers were again turned over as reparations to the victorious nations~ and considerably more valued the second time around. They now serve as naval cadet trainers and are the nucleus of the tall ship fleet throughout the world.

The "Dar Pomorza"~ built in 1910~ 267 feet in length, was an ex-German from World War I. She was turned over to France and later sold to the Polish State Sea Training School. Donations from the province of Pomorza made the transfer possible. "Horst Wessel" (1936, 266 feet) became the pride of the United States Coast Guard (and the United States, for that matter), the "Eagle." She had three close sister ships. One, the ex-German "Gorch Fock I" (1933, 240 feet), was sunk in 1945, then raised by Russia. She was recommissioned as the "Tovarishsch" in 1951. The second, the "Gorch Fock II" (1958, 266 feet), is West Germany's new sail-training replacement. The third sister ship, the "Sagres II" (1937, 268 feet), was damaged by mines in the second World War, passed to America as a reparation payment, and then handed to Brazil. There she saw service as a training ship until 1961, when she was sold to the Portuguese Navy. The German Laeisz "P" Line "Padua" (1926, 342 feet), the last cargo-carrying bark ever built, became the present Russian "Kruzenshtern."

The United States Naval Academy mans a fleet of 130 smaller sailing craft. In addition to the basic training during plebe summer, the Academy encourages intercollegiate competition, ocean racing, and cruise credit.

THE SAIL TRAINING ASSOCIATION

The post-war momentum to preserve our tall ship heritage continues to move ahead with the speed of the old clipper ships. This effort is in a large part due to the young adventurous spirits around the world who are now sailing under the guidance of the Sail Training Association. There are several important goals — "promoting sail training as an educational and character-building experience for young people, bringing together the sailing ships of the world in a spirit of friendship and international goodwill, and educating our young people in the values of our maritime traditions." The program is not designed to produce a generation of yachtsmen or professional seamen.

SAIL TRAINING ASSOCIATION.

It wasn't always so. Britain had long opposed the worth of sail training on the grounds that powered merchantmen crews would resent a sail-trained officer, and dissension aboard might be the unhappy result. But this island of seafarers, conscious of their wealth of maritime heritage, had second thoughts by 1954. An international Sail Training Race was sponsored, and it met with such success in Europe that the Sail Training Association became a permanent organization. Although Britain had no sail training vessels of her own at the time, her enthusiasm has created no less than fourteen sailing associations to date.

AMERICAN SAIL TRAINING ASSOCIATION.

America was a late bloomer. Sail training had been hobbled by restrictive regulations. Trainees were considered the same as long-term crew members ~ and also in the same category as regular passengers. Stiff insurance costs were prohibitive, and the United States could only look with envy at the sail revival going on abroad. None of our craft took part in the races between 1954 and 1972. Then the late Barclay Warburton sailed his own hermaphrodite brig "Black Pearl" across the Atlantic to take part in the 1972 England-to-Germany Sail Training Races. The experience convinced him of the need for an organization similar to the S.T.A. on this side of the ocean. America was soon in the running with the fledgling American Sail Training Association.

The A.S.T.A. was soon working hand in hand with its S.T.A. associate to make the 1976 Bicentennial Tall Ships visit a reality. It was a sight straight out of the pages of history ~ a parade of lofty sea-going nostalgia that captured the imagination of shore-watchers and seafarers alike.

BRITISH SEA CADET CORPS BRIG "ROYALIST"- ONE OF THE GROWING BRITISH FLEET.

AMERICAN REVOLUTION
BICENTENNIAL CELEBRATION-
OPERATION SAIL, 1976.

The American Sail Training Association had brought the best of the old tall ship tradition to these shores, and all Americans responded with a surge of pride in their maritime past. There was a real awareness of what was almost lost~ and what might be gained through training our impressionable youth under sail. This wave of consciousness was evident among our legislators as well. The Sailing School Vessels Act of 1982 became law. Two new classes aboard ship were established~trainees and instructors~with regulations designed to encourage the growth of sailing. The spirit of the law urged guidance for new training programs and sailing school certification from the A.S.T.A., Council of Educational Shipowners, and the Sea Education Association. An optimistic future, indeed!

Of interest is the wide variety of classes offered on shipboard. A sampler would include practical seamanship, such as small boat handling, map and compass, deck work, weather, keeping the log, anchoring, helmsmanship, piloting, rigging, physics of sail and sail handling, safety procedures, use of specialized equipment, engineering systems, and celestial and coastal navigation. Other courses involve sailing maneuvers and racing techniques, meteorology and oceanography, fishing and fisheries management, sea biology, shark tagging, Chesapeake oystering traditions, island ecology, naval architecture and boatbuilding, cultural and historical exploration of countries to be visited, maritime heritage preservation, maritime careers, photography, sea art, sea chanteys, snorkeling, diving, and windsurfing.

Sea Scouts, Girl Scouts, and other youth organizations, college students, learning-disabled groups, paid trainees on for-profit coastal traders, families, and vacationers are among those who have added a new dimension to their lives from such learning experiences.

~ BRIGANTINE "BLACK PEARL"~
RACED IN THE 1972 INTERNATIONAL SAIL-
TRAINING RACE BY BARCLAY WARBURTON
AND LATER DONATED TO THE A.S.T.A..
SHE WAS THEN SOLD TO A NEW
YORK GROUP ASSOCIATED WITH THE
NATIONAL MARITIME HISTORICAL SOCIETY.

LIFE ABOARD

A century and a half ago Richard Dana wrote that "There is a witchery in the sea, its songs and stories, and in the mere sight of a ship and the sailor's dress, especially to a young mind, which has done more to man navies, and fill merchantmen, than all the pressgangs of Europe." He goes on to say that "No sooner, however, has the young sailor begun his life in earnest, than all the fine drapery falls off, and he learns that it is but work and hardship after all."

If Dana could shoulder his duffle bag and ship off into the late twentieth century, he would find life aboard both familiar and strange. Through the years the romantic notions of the sea remain unchanged. He would feel at home with the same salty traditions that he knew – perhaps with a few superstitions added for flavor. The crusty, seawise captain would be there with his mates to insist on heads-up seamanship and pinpoint navigation. And yes – the crew must go about its deck chores if the vessel was to be shipshape and Bristol fashion.

But Dana's old rough-and-tumble mates who sailed the tall ships in the cargo-for-profit days had faded off into the sea mists. In their place are young, bright students – both boys and girls – eager to learn the lessons that life on the sea has to offer. He would find many such surprises aboard the sail-training ships in comparison with the earlier days of sail.

SHIP'S OFFICERS

In Dana's day, the command of a ship might be reached in several ways. The first required that a man pass his twenty-first birthday and have six years of sea duty, one of which must be as first mate. Once by this seasoning process, he was said to have "crawled through the hawse pipes and worked his way aft." On the other hand, one might be "blown through the cabin window." His was the fortunate family who owned or had a heavy number of shares in the ship. Since he had grown up with seafaring in his blood, he would likely have a decent handle on the workings of a ship.

A ship was known by her master. As ruler of his small floating kingdom, his character determined whether life aboard would be a living hell or a happy, rewarding cruise. Many of the packets and some of the down-easters had "Bully" captains – a tough New England breed who were descended from the no-nonsense Puritan days. For them, a fast passage under a press of sail, an efficient and spotless ship, and a profitable cargo at the port of call were reasons enough to drive their crews mercilessly. Woe be to the sailor who slacked off from his duties or practiced poor seamanship. A knuckle dusting would be the answer to anything

c 1850

(OLD DARTMOUTH HISTORICAL SOCIETY, NEW BEDFORD)

CAPTAIN, WITH HIS OUT-SIZED SEXTANT, IS A TRADE FIGURE FROM THE SHOP OF NAUTICAL INSTRUMENT MAKER JAMES FALES OF NEW BEDFORD, MASSACHUSETTS.

less than perfection. Only foreign seamen of uncertain abilities would sign on for this isolated world of stress, and even stricter discipline was the necessary evil.

Fortunately, most masters had a degree of compassion for the frailties of their crew. Such a man would likely avoid profanity, intemperance, and any hint of tyranny ~ and was careful not to ram his version of religion down their throats. "Bible-punching" had no place in a sailor's life ~ he was well enough aware of the nearness of his maker on the last Cape Horn rounding or the next big blow. The welfare and safety of all were the captain's responsibility ~ he must be judge and jury, peacemaker, taskmaster, disciplinarian, champion of the sailors' rights, businessman, accountant, diplomat, physician, expert seaman, and navigator. The quality of the master's leadership could be measured by the number of crewmen signing on for the next voyage.

CAPTAIN WILLIAM CUSHING'S BRASS SPEAKING TRUMPET.
(MAINE MARITIME MUSEUM, BATH)   (SHIPS OF THE SEA, SAVANNAH, GA.)

Basil Lubbock described a case in point. When the crew of the "Frank Pendleton" reached port, they lined up on the wharf and gave three rousing cheers for the ship, three for Captain William Nichols, and three more for their officers. The Maine skipper "was no Nancy* and was far from suffering fools gladly. Neither would he put up with the incompetent nor the slacker but was a prime sailorman whose equal would be hard to find."

Navigation demanded the most of the captain's skills and energies. After the last bearing and distance on landfall, regular recordings of the ship's position by sun, moon, and chronometer were necessary. These observations, along with any workings of the ship or changes in the rigging, were usually made on the weather side of the quarterdeck. This was the master's country, and no man dared to intrude on the sanctity of the place. Respected, feared, imitated, and sometimes hated ~ he led an aloof and lonely life aboard.

There was a solution ~ bring along the family. The Maritime History of Maine reminds us that family life aboard the down-easters was the rule rather than the exception, and likely indeed if the captain owned a controlling interest in the vessel. The cabin was usually decked out with fine wood paneling that was highlighted with gold leaf. Carpets (taken up at sea), easy chairs, and even a piano (all screwed down for safety's sake) gave the living quarters a homey touch.

As for a wife with her pregnancy at term, a midwife might be brought aboard at the next port. If caught mid-ocean, the captain would attend to the matter himself. It was not unusual to name the newcomer after the place of birth ~ Mindoro, Iona, Oceanica, or some such.

The children knew only a hard deck playground instead of a grassy back yard. In their world of adults, they played quietly at their games of dominoes or Authors lest they wake the off-watch below. There was sewing for the girls, and the boys might practice their fancy knot-tying. Reading was always an option, for there was a plentiful supply of books in their fathers'

CAPTAIN DENNY HUMPHREY'S TELESCOPE USED ON THE SHIP "ECLIPSE" FROM 1878 TO 1883 (MAINE MARITIME MUSEUM)
* "NO NANCY" MEANS NOT WEAK OR SOFT.

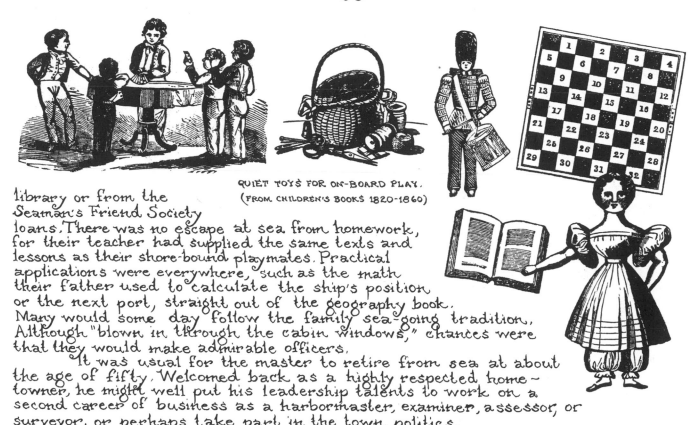

QUIET TOYS FOR ON-BOARD PLAY.
(FROM CHILDREN'S BOOKS 1820-1860)

library or from the
Seaman's Friend Society
loans. There was no escape at sea from homework,
for their teacher had supplied the same texts and
lessons as their shore-bound playmates. Practical
applications were everywhere, such as the math
their father used to calculate the ship's position
or the next port, straight out of the geography book.
Many would some day follow the family sea-going tradition.
Although "blown in through the cabin windows," chances were
that they would make admirable officers.

It was usual for the master to retire from sea at about
the age of fifty. Welcomed back as a highly respected home-
towner, he might well put his leadership talents to work on a
second career of business as a harbormaster, examiner, assessor, or
surveyor, or perhaps take part in the town politics.

Anyone could point out his home. It was the one with the tropical shell
and coral sidewalk border. Once inside, the visitor would be treated to a
museum of momentoes~Japanese screens, teak and sandlewood chests, a camphorwood
desk, and such wonderous furnishings. There might be arrangements of South Sea
bird feathers and a sweep of pampas grass on the mantle. Here and there were
Japanese fans, jungle carvings, scrimshaw, jade, ivory card holders, and even bottles of
volcanic ash. The captain's wife might serve tea from her China tea service along
with the fragrances of ginger and preserved Tamarinds, curry, and guava jelly. Any
visitors would part company with the feeling that they had returned from a
magic carpet cruise around the world.

The merchant marine and maritime academies of today continue the sail training
tradition. A master's license is required of a sea-going skipper-teacher. Naval
captains are usually of that rank, although the commissioned warrant officer is often
considered the unofficial captain of large square-riggers, while ensigns have the
responsibility aboard some of the smaller craft. Since the cruises are shorter
and the schooling so concentrated in that time, the captain's family must stay
shoreside while he is at sea.

MATES ~ The first mate must be at least nineteen years old
with five years of sea service. He was responsible for seeing
that the captain's orders were carried out quickly and
efficiently. Known as "the mate," he was first lieutenant, sailing master, boatswain, and quarter~
master. On the old cargo tall ship,
he took charge of the log book, and
had to answer to the owners and insur-
ers for the stowage, delivery, and safe-
keeping of the cargo.

SCRIMSHAW
OFFICER'S WHISTLE.

(MARITIME MUSEUM,
PHILADELPHIA, PA.)

Memories still linger of the "Bully" captains and their "Bucko" mates bearing down on their heterogeneous packet and down-easter crews. It was said that after the first two weeks at sea, even the most ornery seaman dare not grumble at his lot. Other mates, if not feared, were certainly respected as the captain's right-hand man. Still, it would be best to chuckle at any bit of wit or a joke that he might share with the crew.

BRASS KNUCKLES~ WEAPON OF OFFENSE AND DEFENSE FOR SAILOR ASHORE OR ON LIBERTY. (PEABODY MUSEUM, SALEM)

"THE MATE" TOLERATED NO IDLENESS ABOARD.
(ICONOGRAPHIC ENCYCLOPEDIA, J.G. HECK, 1851)

On the sail training ships, the merchant marine cadets and the Sail Training Association students still know their officers by the same titles. Fortunately, these are men dedicated to teaching, and any heavy-handed tyrants on the old ships have disappeared with time. On naval sailers, a commissioned warrant officer would be the equivalent of the first mate.

The second mate must be at least seventeen years old with four years at sea. No man envied his lot in life, for he had to enforce the captain's orders yet must reef, furl, tar and scrape with the forecastle crowd. Straddling, as he was, between the commander and the commanded, he was shown little respect by either. The boatswain's locker, with its coils of rope, spun-yarn, serving boards, marlinespikes and the like, was his responsibility. He doled out the supplies as needed and was known by the crew as the "sailor's waiter." At least his duties didn't include a turn at the helm~ a small reward indeed. He would have envied the naval training vessels, where his deck duties are now carried out by the chief boatswain's mate with three first-class boatswain's mates to assist him~ one at each mast.

THE "IDLERS"

These were the specialists aboard and were a cut above the seamen~ and hardly idle. They worked through the daylight hours and could usually look forward to a full night's sleep.

THE CARPENTER ("CHIPS") As one would expect, this handyman and make-do artist kept the woodwork shipshape~ decks, spars, boats, interior bulkheads, bunks, and the like. Before sailing, he would seal all the cargo hatches. Less known was his ability to keep all the machinery in order~ steering gear, pumps, windlasses and the anchor lifts. He could do creditable blacksmith repairs in a pinch. It was also his lot to care for the vital fresh water supplies, and could be roused out for watch duty and ordinary deck work during storms.

THE SAILMAKER An expert in canvas, he repaired any sails

THE CARPENTER KEPT SEAMS WATERTIGHT WITH OAKUM, THEN PAYED WITH HOT PITCH.

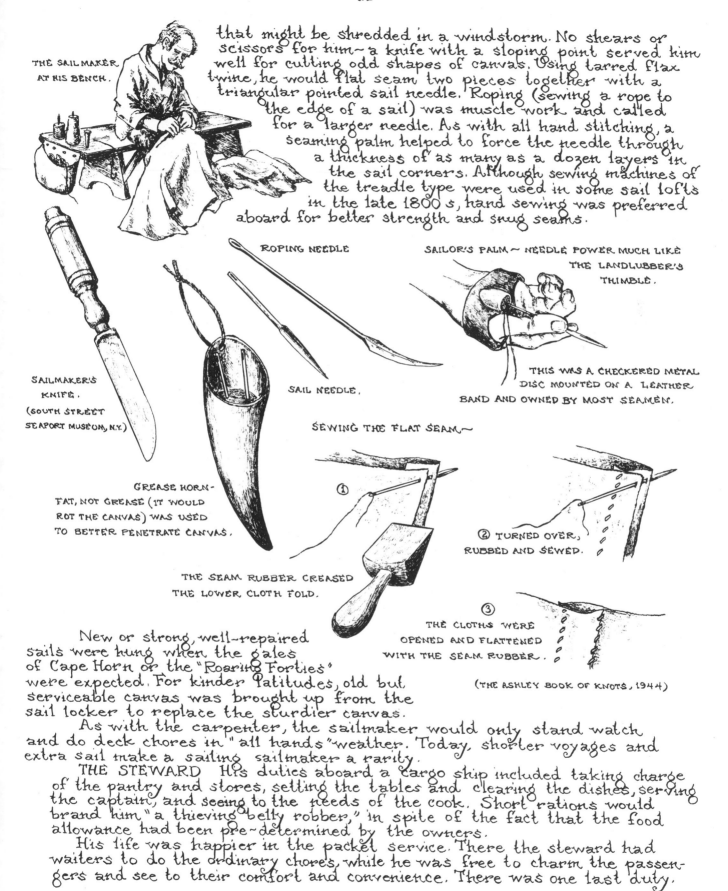

THE SAILMAKER AT HIS BENCH.

that might be shredded in a windstorm. No shears or scissors for him ~ a knife with a sloping point served him well for cutting odd shapes of canvas. Using tarred flax twine, he would flat seam two pieces together with a triangular pointed sail needle. Roping (sewing a rope to the edge of a sail) was muscle-work and called for a larger needle. As with all hand stitching, a seaming palm helped to force the needle through a thickness of as many as a dozen layers in the sail corners. Although sewing machines of the treadle type were used in some sail lofts in the late 1800 s, hand sewing was preferred aboard for better strength and snug seams.

ROPING NEEDLE

SAILOR'S PALM ~ NEEDLE POWER MUCH LIKE THE LANDLUBBER'S THIMBLE.

SAILMAKER'S KNIFE.
(SOUTH STREET SEAPORT MUSEUM, N.Y.)

SAIL NEEDLE.

THIS WAS A CHECKERED METAL DISC MOUNTED ON A LEATHER BAND AND OWNED BY MOST SEAMEN.

GREASE HORN ~ FAT, NOT GREASE (IT WOULD ROT THE CANVAS) WAS USED TO BETTER PENETRATE CANVAS.

SEWING THE FLAT SEAM ~

①

② TURNED OVER, RUBBED AND SEWED.

THE SEAM RUBBER CREASED THE LOWER CLOTH FOLD.

③ THE CLOTHS WERE OPENED AND FLATTENED WITH THE SEAM RUBBER.

(THE ASHLEY BOOK OF KNOTS, 1944)

New or strong, well-repaired sails were hung when the gales of Cape Horn or the "Roaring Forties" were expected. For kinder latitudes, old but serviceable canvas was brought up from the sail locker to replace the sturdier canvas.

As with the carpenter, the sailmaker would only stand watch and do deck chores in "all hands" weather. Today, shorter voyages and extra sail make a sailing sailmaker a rarity.

THE STEWARD His duties aboard a cargo ship included taking charge of the pantry and stores, setting the tables and clearing the dishes, serving the captain, and seeing to the needs of the cook. Short rations would brand him "a thieving belly robber," in spite of the fact that the food allowance had been pre-determined by the owners.

His life was happier in the packet service. There the steward had waiters to do the ordinary chores, while he was free to charm the passengers and see to their comfort and convenience. There was one last duty.

He saw to it that the cargo hatches were secured in heavy seas.

THE COOK His castle was his galley, and his badge of honor the smeared apron that gave many a hint of previous menus. On a packet, he might wear a white jacket, and his apron had lost its abstract painting effect. He who was befriended by the cook could share the warmth of the galley stove or dry out after a stormy watch. As with the steward, there was no watch duty, but he was expected to help on deck in emergencies. No seamanship was expected of him.

SHIP'S MAHOGANY CHOPPING BOWL.
(MARINER'S MUSEUM, NEWPORT NEWS, VA.)

While the merchant marine sail trainers continue the same names for idlers, naval sail carried them under different titles. For example, on the United States Coast Guard "Eagle," a chief petty officer is cook with nine assistants to service the cabin wardroom and general mess. With reasonably calm seas, hungry cadets have need of this number of food handlers. Other idler specialists coping with the complexities of life aboard the "Eagle" are a lieutenant junior grade supply officer, a yeoman, chief quartermaster as an electronic technician, and a first-class radarman. The old time carpenter would be amazed at the number of men that saw to his work. Advanced engineering requires a warrant machinist, a chief petty officer machinist technician, three engineering petty officers, two electrician mates, two carpenter's mates for damage control, and four firemen!

SHIP'S CREW

ABLE SEAMAN ~ Hand a man a serving mallet and point him toward some standing rigging in need of repair. He'll soon enough prove his worth as an able seaman by worming, parceling, and servicing. He is skilled in making chafing gear, doing fancy knots, reeving running rigging, and reefing, furling, and setting sail.

① WORMING WITH A SERVING MALLET FILLED ROPE GROVES WITH SMALL CORDAGE TO KEEP OUT MOISTURE.

(ALL FROM "ASHLEY BOOK OF KNOTS" 1944)

② PARCELING ~ AFTER WORMING, STRIPS OF TAR-SOAKED CANVAS ARE WRAPPED UPWARDS FOR A SHINGLING EFFECT TO KEEP OUT MOISTURE.

BAGGYWRINKLE ~ A WRAPPING OF FRAYED ROPE TO PREVENT THE RIGGING FROM CHAFING THE CANVAS.

A SERVING BOARD IS USED FOR EYES.

SERVING MALLET.

③ SERVICE ~ THE ROPE IS TIGHTLY BOUND WITH SMALL CORDAGE TO PROTECT IT FROM WEATHER.

WORMING, PARCELING, AND SERVICE FOR STANDING RIGGING ARE ALWAYS PUT ON WITH MATERIALS WELL SOAKED IN TAR.

Because of his experience, he was positioned at the most important running rigging when handling sail, steered the ship, and was expected to be able to coxswain one of the ship's boats.

ORDINARY SEAMEN ~ Although unskilled at rigging work or managing the helm, he was expected to tie the commonly used knots, understand the functions of the standing and running rigging, and be able to set or furl a sail.

A short-lived 1817 law required that two thirds of an American vessel be citizens. It was quite unworkable~ the growing packet trade saw to that. No right-thinking Yankee lad had any intention of living out months in the forecastle of such a ship. Rigid schedules, valuable cargo, and distinguished passengers called for record-setting passages. Foul weather or no, every thread of canvas was aloft to catch the winds. The heavy single topsails and the constant tacking drove the deck hands to exhaustion. In this small world of turmoil and danger, there were but twenty or so deck hands who had to be driven to push the packet beyond any reasonable limit.

Under such conditions, at least three quarters of the crew were foreign born. These were the "packet rats"~ the dregs of any waterfront where the packet docked. Shiftless, unscrupulous, and strangers to soap, they spent aimless lives in cheap boarding houses. Sooner or later, the house-keeper would slosh them with hard liquor and herd them aboard for a price. This was the heavy-handed art of crimping, and it filled many a ship in the nineteenth century. Once shanghaied, the bulk of the crew would jump ship at the next port. The crimps, ever ready to be of service, hid the fugitives until their ship left harbor. Out came the hard spirits for another drinking spree. Semi-stuporous, the "rats" would be pushed or dragged off to another ship that was short-handed and ready to sail. Masters would pay upwards of one hundred dollars a head to those same crimps who had encouraged desertion from their own vessels.

Whaling ships, with their interminable voyages, heavy work, and wretched living conditions, offered little enticement to seamen. The "spouters" cheerfully signed on any restless spirit who was tired of farming or millwork, as well as adventurers, drunkards, escaped criminals, town misfits, and runaways. Fortunately, there were also those bright, self-respecting lads from the seacoast towns who had grown up with the traditions of whaling in their blood. They would rise above the forecastle riffraff and one day command a vessel of their own. Perhaps they would become the "bully" captains and "bucko" mates with the stern discipline necessary to keep the heterogeneous crew in line.

The California clippers were no bargains when it came to crews. Many of their number shipped aboard as a way to get to the gold fields. They were a rough and tough bunch~ trouble-makers who had but one good point. They could be counted on to desert the moment the ship was dockside. Short-handed or not when the clipper set sail for China, all hands could look forward to better days.

A native-born young man, wishing to

CERAMIC TAR STOVE. TAR MELTED IN A SHALLOW BUCKET ⬤ THAT RESTED ON TOP; THE FIRE WAS IN THE LOWER CHAMBER.

(MAINE MARITIME MUSEUM, BATH)

① MARLINESPIKE WITH A KNOBBED HEAD FOR POUNDING. USED FOR TIGHTENING SERVICE, OPENING ROPE STRANDS FOR KNOTTING AND SPLICING.

②+③ FIDS~ HEADS DO NOT BULGE, LIKE THE MARLINSPIKE, BEYOND THE LINE OF THE CONE'S TAPER. USED FOR ROUNDING OUT EYES IN ROPE AND EYES IN SAILCLOTH.

(AFTER "ASHLEY'S BOOK OF KNOTS," 1944)

FOC'SLE OF THE WHALER "CHARLES W. MORGAN" PRESERVED AT THE MYSTIC SEAPORT MUSEUM.

follow the sea, would set his sights on a "happy" ship. Along the shore-line, word of mouth traveled faster than a squall, and a considerate captain and evenhanded mates had little difficulty filling the crew's quarters. A seaman would make no mistake if he signed on one of the earlier down-easters. Family owned and captained, their medium clipper officers usually took a fair measure of a man's worth. Unfortunately, the increased competition and decline of sail in the late 1800s dropped many a ship to the level of a hard-driven packet. Ambitious young men turned to a more rewarding life ashore and might well follow the western land migration for their own piece of America. Late European medium clippers suffered from the same disenchantment.

The permanent crews on today's sail trainers have passed standardized written and practical examinations for their ratings. Beyond this, the specifics of square-rigged sailing are learned from experienced hands and such books as <u>Eagle Seamanship ~ A Manual for Square Rigger Sailing</u>. These professionals have certainly upgraded the old forecastle days and help provide the cadets with their hands-on learning.

BOYS ~ Here at the bottom of the ship's ladder were the "boys" ~ any green hand shipping aboard regardless of age. He lacked all manner of seamanship skills but would learn such basics as drawing and pulling yarns (a number of rope fibers twisted together), sinnets and its various forms of braiding and simple knots. He must be at the able seaman's elbow and be ready to lend a hand. Sweeping and cleaning the decks, holding the log reel, coiling the rigging ropes, and loosening and furling the light sails were part of his day. He stood watches with those more experienced and would join in the "all hands" call to fur'l and do other deck duties.

THAT FIRST DAY ABOARD

THE COMMON SINNET ~ THE SIMPLEST OF BRAIDING AND KNOWN TO EVERY SCHOOL GIRL WITH PIGTAILS.

The boy's first day was one of bewilderment. Trying to keep from underfoot, he wondered at the confusion of rigging and the swarms of men that seemed to hang by their heels from it. The dock was fast fading in the distance, and tears came easily. The sea chest that held his worldly possessions was his only bond to the family he left behind. It was a lonely, depressing prospect to be a know-nothing among this company of strangers. At least there were other boys aboard (for example, the clipper ship "Sovereign of the Seas" carried ten boys to assist the eighty able-bodied seamen). Hard work, new friendships, basic seamanship being practiced wherever the eye is cast, and the prospect of high adventure could help him grow up rapidly in this man's world.

A BOY TIMES THE LOG ~ A WEIGHTED WOODEN BOARD ~ AS ITS LINE WAS RUN OUT ASTERN. THE NUMBER OF KNOTS IN THE LINE THAT PASSED IN ONE MINUTE WAS THE SPEED OF THE SHIP. (ICONOGRAPHIC ENCYCLOPEDIA, 1851)

The green boys and the apprentices on past cargo square-riggers have been replaced by mature cadets on today's sail trainers. Although a few ships, such as the Danish merchant "Georg Stage," accept physically fit and able young men at fourteen to fifteen and a half years of age, most of these future merchant and naval officers average between twenty and twenty-five years. They leave the academy classrooms with a solid background of navigational and seamanship theories. None have been to sea before, and they start the practical application of their book learning on an equal footing. As classmates and not strangers, the cadets may enter the world of square sails with a measure of confidence that was unknown to the boys of earlier days.

Each cadet has his own locker for his issued uniforms and another for boots and shoes. Each is assigned a number for mess table seating and a position at the rigging. With so many cadets aboard ~ on the "Eagle", he is one of a hundred and seventy trainees along with fifty-seven permanent hands ~ drills by the numbering system rather than by names work most efficiently. Number assignments are changed frequently to give a broad working knowledge of the ship. There are exercises to keep the crew limber. "Jumping Jacks" could be a novel experience on a rolling deck. The landing might be some distance from the starting point.

The first day of the shakedown cruise would include a welcome and general thoughts by the captain. The stocky, seventy-year-old master of the "Christian Radich," according to one cadet's diary, summed up the advice given on many a sailing ship. "Training you to become good sailors is the primary mission of this cruise. All of you have been hand-picked and we expect you to live up to our requirements. All you have to do is obey orders and do your duty like men. If we pull together you will find me a decent fellow; if we don't, you will find me something quite different."

The entry-level trainee would do well to follow the lead of the upper classmen. They usually handled the duties of the ship's officers and could pass on their know-how to the green hands. More formal classroom teaching would be held both morning and afternoon. Between sessions, it was learning by doing. The cadet could count on practicing his seamanship, navigation, Rules of the Road, watch duties, lifeboat drill, and engine safety. That first climb up the ratlines would be a challenge and a half. No one need repeat the rule "One hand for the ship, and one for yourself." When one hundred and forty or more feet up, on a mast that cuts wide arcs through the air, and looking down on a distant, plunging deck,

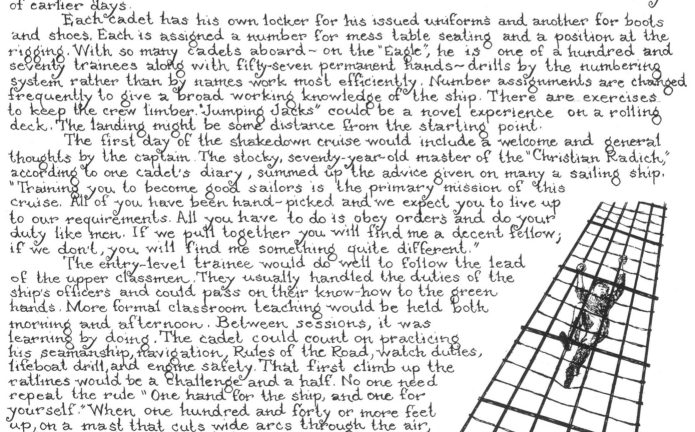

one's stomach would rather be elsewhere. Yet, doing one's part in furling a wildly flapping sail could give an immense sense of satisfaction and accomplishment.

All this was soon to come. Meanwhile, the first evening aboard ended with the hammocks being hung (the "Eagle" is an exception, for she has the luxury of bunks). Climbing onto this canvas pendulum without capsizing might take a few attempts. Space on a windjammer is at a premium, and hammocks are stowed when not in use.

TRAINING CRUISES

Cruises might last as long as nine months. The Portuguese naval school ship "Sagres" takes a three- to a four-month run to Rio de Janeiro and Buenos Aires or New York and New Bedford with stop-overs at Madeira, the Cape Verdes, and the Azores. The merchant school ship "Danmark" extends her voyage to eight or nine months, also calling on the Cape Verde Islands and continuing on to the West Indies and ports along the Gulf of Mexico. In 1981, the "Eagle" was off on a transatlantic cruise from New London, Connecticut, that included South Ireland, Lisbon, Portugal, Malaga, Spain, the Grand Canarys, Bermuda, Newport, Rhode Island, and then back to her home port. Four years later, she saw a good bit of the North American coastline, with ports of call at Bermuda, Cape Canaveral, Florida, Mobile, Alabama, Jacksonville, Florida, Norfolk, Virginia, Boston, St. Pierre and Miquelon Islands, and then back to New London by way of Gloucester, Boston, and New Bedford.

The "Sørlandet" is the oldest existing Norwegian-built square-rigger and has been in service since 1927. She is the only full-rigged ship in the world available for crew participation by the general public. Through the efforts of Square-Rig International— a non-profit organization from the United States, Canada, and Bermuda, the "Sørlandet" commemorated the fiftieth anniversary of her passage to the 1933 World's Fair at Chicago. Her similar cruise in 1983 was divided into four separate sail training segments. The first began at Bermuda, stopped over at Boston, and ended in Quebec. The second leg took her from Quebec for a three-week cruise up the St. Lawrence Seaway with stops at Chicago, Duluth, and Thunder Bay. The third segment carried her from Thunder Bay, through the Great Lakes, down the St. Lawrence to Halifax, Nova Scotia. Lastly, the "Sørlandet" sailed from there to Bermuda, with a stop at Newport, Rhode Island. The ship's company consisted of seventeen permanent Norwegian crew and

ATLANTIC OCEAN

SOME SAIL TRAINING SHIPS' PORTS OF CALL.

NORWEGIAN SØRLANDET.

seventy international cadets~including family members sixteen years or older.
Life on the training cruises wasn't all work and study. Not quite. There was sightseeing at each port of call (afoot on shore could give a strange sensation of land in motion for those with their sea legs). There were times to relax with movies, radio, writing letters, catching forty winks, or the usual scuttlebutt. On the Spanish "Juan Sebastian" there were nightly concerts by twenty musicians playing both classical Spanish and modern tunes. Touches of home comforts aboard the sail trainers might be the smell of fresh bread baking in the electric ovens. Fresh meat and produce could outlast extended passages in the cold storage, for all modern sailing ships carry generators. This home away from home has electric lights and perhaps air conditioning, electric irons to de-wrinkle uniforms, and salt water showers to follow the deck duties. Mothering, however, is not included.

YOUNG WOMEN ~ It would be a mistake to carry away the impression that square-rigged sailing is an experience for men only. Mentioned earlier were the many American and Scandinavian masters who had their wives aboard. Women were usually crew members on short-haul Baltic sailers. Some of the later Finnish cargo vessels signed on few as cadets or stewardesses. Ten percent of the United States Coast Guard "Eagle's" crew are women. The need for separate quarters prompted the change from hammocks to bunks. On the American Sail Training Association vessels, girls make up a large proportion of the trainees. The "Sir Winston Churchill" was built in 1966 specifically to represent Great Britain in the Tall Ship Races. She carried an all-girl crew on the Bermuda-to-Newport leg of the Tall Ship's Race ten years later. Britain was the first nation to encourage young women to become crew members on the Sail Training vessels.

When the seasoned cadet takes leave of his or her sail-training adventure, each is part of the ancient marine brotherhood who have met the challenges of the sea under sail.

YOUNG WOMEN TRAINEES ABOARD THE
A.S.T.A. BRIGANTINE "BLACK PEARL" OUT OF NEWPORT, RHODE ISLAND.

CLOTHING

Merchant marine officers wore no distinguishing clothing, unless they sailed for one of the large shipping lines.

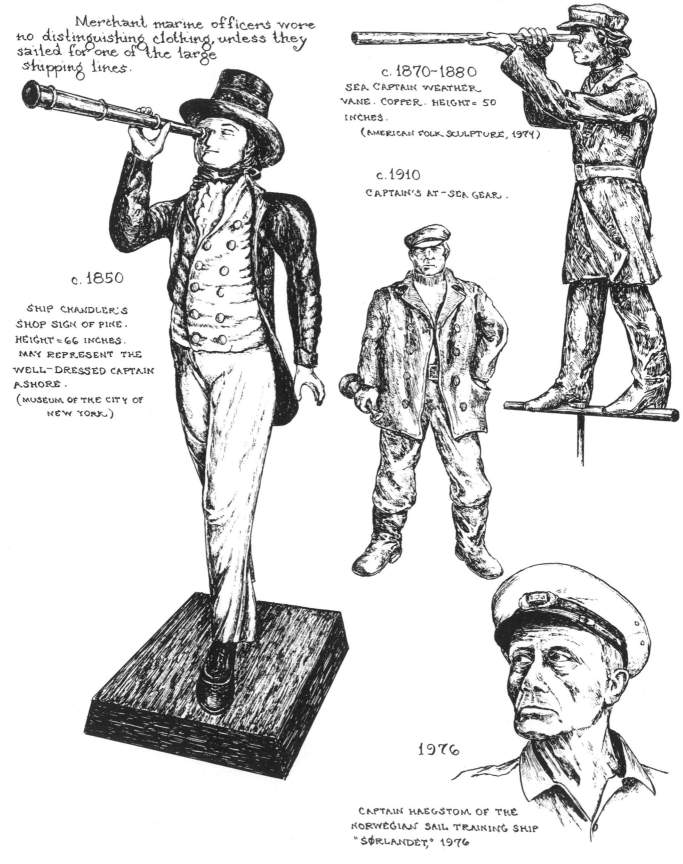

c.1870-1880

SEA CAPTAIN WEATHER VANE. COPPER. HEIGHT = 50 INCHES.

(AMERICAN FOLK SCULPTURE, 1974)

c.1910

CAPTAIN'S AT-SEA GEAR.

c.1850

SHIP CHANDLER'S SHOP SIGN OF PINE. HEIGHT = 66 INCHES. MAY REPRESENT THE WELL-DRESSED CAPTAIN ASHORE.

(MUSEUM OF THE CITY OF NEW YORK.)

1976

CAPTAIN HAEGSTOM OF THE NORWEGIAN SAIL TRAINING SHIP "SØRLANDET," 1976

DECKING OUT THE SEAMAN~

No one could mistake the sailor ashore. His distinctive dress was much like that of the navy ~ tradition and practicality were woven into every fiber. The experienced sea rover wore his outfit with style, and green hands would find it difficult to imitate their natty appearance.

HATS ~ since the eighteenth century, the tarpaulin hat was the seaman's pride. The broad brim gave a decent runoff of the drizzle, and tar and oil kept it black, glossy, and waterproof. Before going ashore, half a fathom (three feet) of black ribbon would be tied in a bow about the crown. Its tails would hang over the left eye. In 1890 the tarpaulin was discontinued by the Royal Navy, and few were seen in the merchant service after that date.

c.1840
TARPAULIN HAT.
(PEABODY MUSEUM OF SALEM.

During the second half of the nineteenth century, several navies and some commercial crewmen preferred a leather hat. Its ribbon was knotted so that the tails would hang over the back of the head.

c.1870
LEATHER HAT.

The sennit hat was a braided straw version of the tarpaulin hat and was a must for the tropics. Popular throughout the 1800s, it was very much in evidence in photographs of the 1930s.

Scotch caps are mentioned in contemporary merchant tall ship accounts since the early nineteenth century. Both the Confederate and Union naval seamen were issued versions of this headgear during the Civil War. Those of us who entered World War II as apprentice seamen continued the modified scotch cap tradition as part of our dress uniforms. The British and other navies still do so.

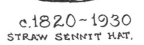

c.1820~1930
STRAW SENNIT HAT.

c.1860

CIGAR STORE SAILOR.
(NEW YORK HISTORICAL SOCIETY)

A SCOTCH-CAPPED SAILOR IN LEG IRONS
PASSES TIME FASHIONING A STRAW SENNIT HAT.
(ICONOGRAPHIC ENCYCLOPEDIA, J. G. HECK, 1851)

The what-ever dress of square-rigger crewmen after the 1880s mirrored the general decline of sail. Foreign sailors with varied talents made up most of the forecastle hands. Visored caps were frequently seen in old photographs.

EARLY 1900s.

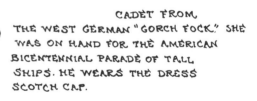

1900~1940
Sail training ships carried on the traditions of the sea. This Danish lad was one of the forty-five cadets lost at sea when the "København" sank with all hands in 1929. He wears the scotch cap.
(FROM PHOTO, THE "COMPASS". 1984~NO.2)

1976

RUSSIAN CADET, WITH SCOTCH
CAP, FROM THE "KRUZENSHTERN."
AMERICAN BICENTENNIAL CELEBRATION.

1976

CADET FROM
THE WEST GERMAN "GORCH FOCK." SHE
WAS ON HAND FOR THE AMERICAN
BICENTENNIAL PARADE OF TALL
SHIPS. HE WEARS THE DRESS
SCOTCH CAP.

1980s

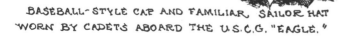

BASEBALL-STYLE CAP AND FAMILIAR SAILOR HAT
WORN BY CADETS ABOARD THE U.S.C.G. "EAGLE."

THE STOCKING CAP SAW SEA DUTY
FROM THE EARLIEST DAYS OF SAIL AND REMAINS
POPULAR FOR WINTRY DECK DUTY.

NECKERCHIEF ~ This neckwear was originally used as a sweat band around the neck, and not, as some would have us believe, to honor the death of Nelson. Always black, it nicely masked any tar stains or other soiling. It was tied in a square knot. This traditional neckwear continues to be worn with the broad-collared shirt.

SHIRTS ~ Eighteenth-century sailors wore their hair in a pigtail that was doubled back on itself, or "clubbed." The pigtail was then tarred, and he was known as "Jack Tar" thereafter. Since tar can make some nasty smudges on one's monkey jacket, a broad extension from the back of the shirt collar solved the problem. Sail-training cadets today still wear this distinctive feature of their seagoing ancestors.

While a white cotton, broad-collared shirt might be worn by a fortunate nineteenth-century crewman ashore, the odds-on favorite was a cotton checked shirt in either blue or red. It was perfectly acceptable as dress or work-a-day wear, and most crewmen had several.

Richard Dana had the luxury of six such. There was no skimping of material, and this superabundance gave no restriction of movement. Still, a few more yards and it would seem a perfectly good checkered substitute for a main sail!

1980 s - CADET'S BROAD COLLAR. GERMANY'S "GORCH FOCK."

WORN ALL PERIODS.

SEAMAN'S CHECKERED SHIRT.

1846

STRIPED SHIRT WORN BY A SAILOR ON SIR JOHN FRANKLIN'S ILL-FATED EXPEDITION IN 1846 TO FIND A NORTHWEST PASSAGE.

1820~1900 THE POPULAR JERSEY ~ A WARM WOOLEN SWEATER FIRST WORN BY JERSEY ISLAND FISHERMEN ~ WAS COLD WEATHER GEAR. A RED FLANNEL SHIRT AND LONG UNDERPANTS HELPED FEND OFF THE CAPE HORN CHILLS.

1820~80 THE GUERNSEY WAS A SNUG WOOL SHIRT OFTEN WORN BY SEAMEN, AND WAS FIRST USED BY SEAMEN ON THE ISLAND OF GUERNSEY. DUNGAREES OF BLUE DENIM FITTED TIGHTLY AT THE HIPS BUT BELLED OUT AT THE FEET, THEY COULD BE EASILY ROLLED UP FOR DECK WASHING OR QUICKLY REMOVED IF THE OWNER FELL OVERBOARD.

STOUT COWHIDE BOOTS WERE COVERED WITH A THICK MIXTURE OF MELTED GREASE AND TAR.

1820~80 BLUE JACKET.

1820~1870 DUCK FROCKS WERE MADE FROM OLD SHIP'S CANVAS AND WORN WHEN TARRING THE RIGGING. THEY WERE "DEEP SIXED" WHEN RETURNING HOME.

1830 MASSACHUSETTS BUSK OF WHALEBONE (A SPERM WHALE'S JAW). NOTE BLUE JACKET ("PEA" OR "MONKEY" JACKET). HERE, PANTS HAVE A BUTTONED FLAP ~ OTHERS MIGHT HAVE A BUTTONED OPENING.
(NEW BEDFORD WHALING MUSEUM)

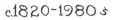
c.1820-1980s

OILED CLOTH "SOU'WESTER" HAT
WITH FLANNEL LINING.
(MYSTIC SEAPORT MUSEUM)

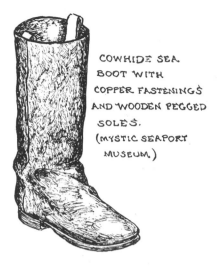

COWHIDE SEA
BOOT WITH
COPPER FASTENINGS
AND WOODEN PEGGED
SOLES.
(MYSTIC SEAPORT
MUSEUM)

OIL SKIN (OIL CLOTH) SUIT OF TARPAULIN ~
IT WAS GIVEN A THOROUGH SOAKING OF
OIL OR TAR AND DRIED. THE SAILOR
USUALLY MADE THE SUIT HIMSELF AND LINED
IT WITH FLANNEL FOR COLD WEATHER.

SHOES

c.1820-1875±
DRESS CALF PUMPS.
(FROM N. CURRIER, 1865,
"BRANDING SLAVES,"
LITHOGRAPH.

(MYSTIC SEAPORT
MUSEUM)

c.1820-1880
HEMP WHALING SHOES,
WORN TO PREVENT SLIPPING
WHILE STANDING ON A WHALE WHEN CUTTING OFF BLUBBER.

c.1960-80s

DECK CANVAS SHOES ~
LIGHT, INEXPENSIVE, AND GRIP A WET
DECK OR ROPE WELL. ISSUED BY
MANY NAVAL AND MERCHANT SAIL
TRAINING SHIPS.

c.1960s-1980s

BOAT MOCCASIN. WATERPROOF WITH NON-
SKID RUBBER SOLES, IT IS FAVORED BY MANY
AMERICAN SAIL TRAINING ASSOCIATION
TRAINEES.

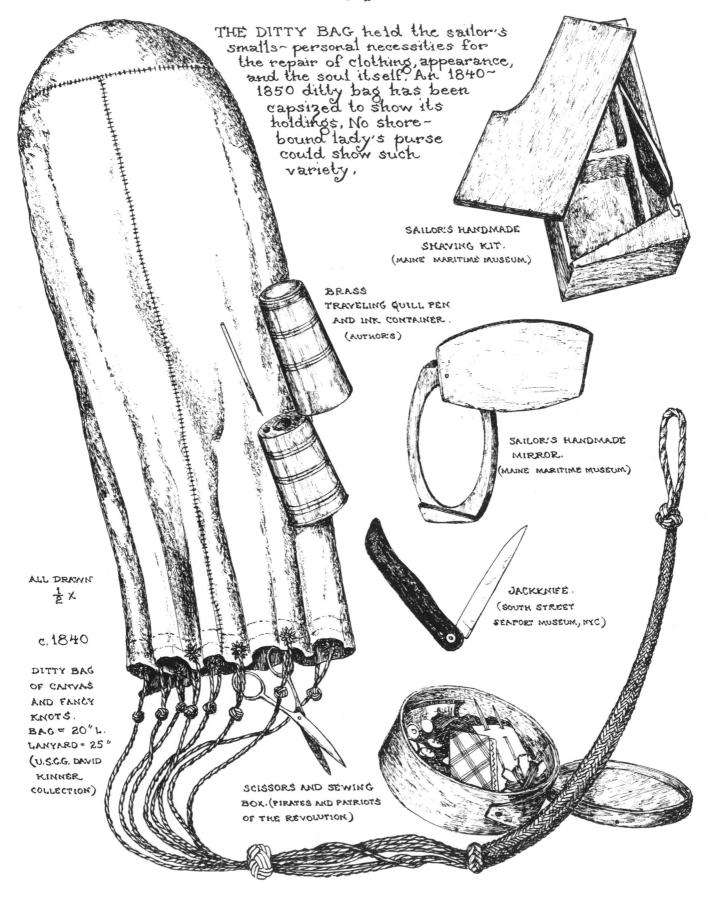

THE DITTY BAG held the sailor's smalls~ personal necessities for the repair of clothing, appearance, and the soul itself. An 1840~ 1850 ditty bag has been capsized to show its holdings. No shore-bound lady's purse could show such variety.

SAILOR'S HANDMADE SHAVING KIT. (MAINE MARITIME MUSEUM.)

BRASS TRAVELING QUILL PEN AND INK CONTAINER. (AUTHOR'S)

SAILOR'S HANDMADE MIRROR. (MAINE MARITIME MUSEUM.)

JACKKNIFE. (SOUTH STREET SEAPORT MUSEUM, NYC)

ALL DRAWN ½ X

c. 1840

DITTY BAG OF CANVAS AND FANCY KNOTS. BAG = 20" L. LANYARD = 25" (U.S.C.G. DAVID KINNER COLLECTION)

SCISSORS AND SEWING BOX. (PIRATES AND PATRIOTS OF THE REVOLUTION)

THE
NEW TESTAMENT
OF OUR
LORD AND SAVIOUR
JESUS CHRIST:
TRANSLATED OUT OF
The Original Greek;
AND WITH
THE FORMER TRANSLATIONS DILIGENTLY
COMPARED AND REVISED.
——
NORTHAMPTON:
PUBLISHED BY J. H. BUTLER.

THE HOLY FAMILY.

1851
ACTUAL SIZE OF
POCKET BIBLE AND
BOOKMARK.
(NORTHAMPTON HISTORICAL
SOCIETY, MASSACHUSETTS.)

SOCIETIES, SUCH AS THE AMERICAN SEAMEN'S
FRIEND SOCIETY, DISTRIBUTED MINI-BIBLES
FOR EASY POCKET OR DITTY BAG CARRYING.

THE SHEATH KNIFE would never keep company with the rest of the ditty bag gear. Emergencies knew no schedule, and so it was sheathed at the middle of the back where it could be quickly reached by either hand. Falling spars and tangled rigging on a wild, rain-swept night called for a decent length of sharp blade—and no pocket knife could answer to that.

½ X

LEATHER SHEATH
WITH BELT SLOTS.
(PEABODY MUSEUM OF
SALEM)

(THE ASHLEY
BOOK OF KNOTS)

(SOUTH STREET SEAPORT
MUSEUM, N.Y.C.)

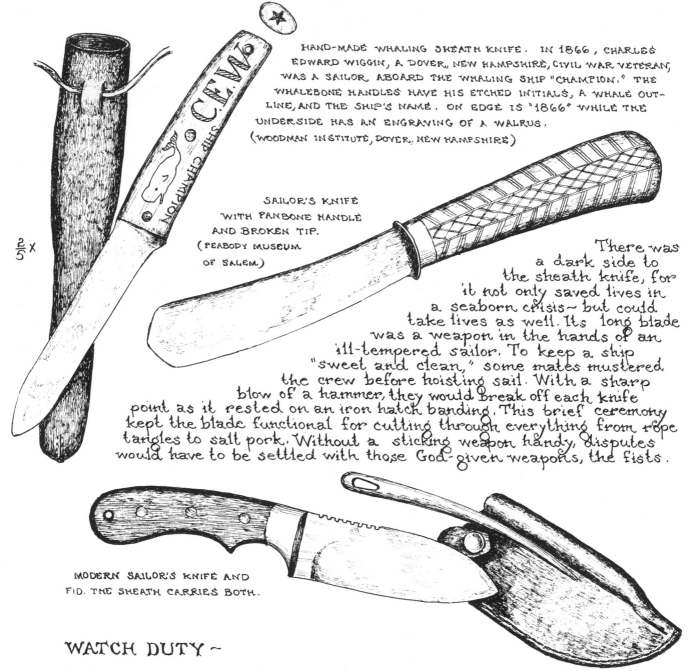

HAND-MADE WHALING SHEATH KNIFE. IN 1866, CHARLES EDWARD WIGGIN, A DOVER, NEW HAMPSHIRE, CIVIL WAR VETERAN, WAS A SAILOR ABOARD THE WHALING SHIP "CHAMPION." THE WHALEBONE HANDLES HAVE HIS ETCHED INITIALS, A WHALE OUTLINE, AND THE SHIP'S NAME. ON EDGE IS "1866" WHILE THE UNDERSIDE HAS AN ENGRAVING OF A WALRUS. (WOODMAN INSTITUTE, DOVER, NEW HAMPSHIRE)

SAILOR'S KNIFE WITH PANBONE HANDLE AND BROKEN TIP. (PEABODY MUSEUM OF SALEM)

$\frac{2}{5}$ X

There was a dark side to the sheath knife, for it not only saved lives in a seaborn crisis ~ but could take lives as well. Its long blade was a weapon in the hands of an ill-tempered sailor. To keep a ship "sweet and clean," some mates mustered the crew before hoisting sail. With a sharp blow of a hammer, they would break off each knife point as it rested on an iron hatch banding. This brief ceremony kept the blade functional for cutting through everything from rope tangles to salt pork. Without a sticking weapon handy, disputes would have to be settled with those God-given weapons, the fists.

MODERN SAILOR'S KNIFE AND FID. THE SHEATH CARRIES BOTH.

WATCH DUTY ~

Before getting underway, "the mate" assembled the crew topside for their watch assignments. Much like choosing sides for one of today's pickup sandlot football games, the first mate cast a practiced eye over the lot. He would beckon to the most likely seaman among them ~ the first to be picked for the port watch. Under this officer's direction, he would be part of the team responsible for keeping the port (left) side of the square-rigger shipshape, as well as the foremast canvas and any gear forward of it.

The second mate, heading up the starboard watch, then had his pick of the rest of the forecastle crowd. His watch was accountable for the condition of the starboard (right) side of the ship, as well as any gear aloft that was aft of the foremast. And so the watch selection continued between the two mates until the least experienced and least promising greenhorn had rounded out the watch list.

A spirit of rivalry between the two watches didn't take long to surface, and a fair deal of joshing could liven routine deck chores. Not only that, but any hint of sloppy seamanship would certainly label a watch as second best.

Life aboard ship revolved around these four-hour watches. It was four hours on deck duty, then four hours off for sack time ~ with one exception. The 4 P.M. ~ 8 P.M. stint was divided into the first and second dog watch, each lasting two hours. This gave a different watch schedule for the following day so that the port and starboard watches covered the same hours every two days. For example:

WATCH DUTY	HOURS ON	DECK WORK
PORT WATCH (STARBOARD THE FOLLOWING DAY)	4 P.M. TO 6 P.M. (1600-1800 HOURS)	~FIRST DOG WATCH. HELM MANNED, LOOKOUT POSTED, SAIL SHORTENED, AND SHIP MADE READY FOR THE NIGHT. 6 P.M. = EVENING MEAL.
	8 P.M. TO 12 MIDNIGHT (2000-2400 HOURS)	~HELM MANNED, LOOKOUT POSTED, WATCH ON DECK WITHIN EASY CALL. NAPPING IN GOOD WEATHER, BRACING OR FURLING SAILS IN DIRTY WEATHER.
	4 A.M. TO 8 A.M. (0400-0800 HOURS)	~HELM AND LOOKOUT, SCRUB DECK, SPREAD SAIL, MAKE PREPARATIONS FOR DAYLIGHT SAILING. 8 A.M. = BREAKFAST. 11:30 A.M. = MIDDAY MEAL.
	12 NOON TO 4 P.M. (1200-1600 HOURS)	~HELM AND LOOKOUT, PAINT, REPAIR, RIGGING, AND GENERAL DECK WORK.
STARBOARD WATCH (PORT WATCH THE FOLLOWING DAY)	6 P.M. TO 8 P.M. (1800-2000 HOURS)	5:30 P.M. = EVENING MEAL. ~SECOND DOG WATCH. HELM AND LOOKOUT, AT EASE.
	12 MIDNIGHT TO 4 AM. (2400-0400 HOURS)	~HELM AND LOOKOUT, REST ON DECK IF WITHIN EASY CALL IN CALM WEATHER. STORMY = NO REST FOR THE WEARY. 7:30 A.M. = BREAKFAST.
	8 A.M. TO 12 NOON (0800-1200 HOURS)	~HELM AND LOOKOUT, PAINTING, SCRAPING, SCRUBBING, AND THE USUAL DECK CHORES. 12:00 NOON = MIDDAY MEAL.

Whatever else the watch must do during its four hours on, manning the helm and lookout posts were musts. Generally they were spelled every hour. In addition, the watch must have a "policeman." He must keep the binnacle (the box near the helm containing the compass) lamps in good order and lit at dusk. His was the unpopular job of rousing out the next watch on time. He must also answer every blast of the mate's whistle. One blast would bring him on the run. Two blasts would call in the entire duty watch. Three blasts meant trouble, and every crew member must tumble topside as the "policeman" yelled "All hands!"

Understandably, the "All hands" call superseded the usual on~off schedule. Jack might face the elements for hours on end, and then find his watch was due, just as the ship had been secured against sea and storm.

ANCHOR WATCH ~ Instead of a watch on deck and the other below, as at sea, all hands worked through the daylight hours, breaking only for meals. At night, the anchor watch kept but two men up and awake as watchmen. The entire crew took turns - infrequently enough to guarantee a full night's sleep.

Because of the outsized cadet crews aboard today's sail-training ships, generally three rather than two watches are in rotation. Therefore a watch would have twelve hours' duty one day and then but six for the following two days. There continues the usual deck housekeeping by day as on earlier tall ships and perhaps such unpleasantries as the night spud-peeling detail. As for those two days with short six-hour watches - the remaining six were filled with class instruction and drills. Hardly a luxury cruise!

TIME BY THE BELL

Time at sea was marked by the number of clangs on the ship's bell - or rather bells, for there were two aboard every merchant square-rigger. The smaller of the two hung abaft the steering wheel. When the nearby ship's clock struck on the half and the full hour, the helmsman would repeat the same number of rings on the bell behind him. The larger bell, located forward in the forecastle country, was struck the same number by any nearby crewman. In response, the lookout would cry out, according to the number of bells struck, "Three bells and all's well. Lights burning bright, Sir!" (The only lights visible above deck before stern lights were required at the turn of this century were the binnacle light and the two navigation lights—red on the port and green on the starboard. The tall ship was a dark sea monster by night.)

Since life aboard revolved around the four-hour watch schedule, it is not surprising that time was divided the same way. When the first half hour of the watch was over, the bell was rung once. The passing of an hour called for two bells. After an hour and a half, three clangs were struck - and so on until eight bells marked the changing of the watch. For example, the 8:00 P.M. to midnight watch would hear these bells and they would be repeated for each watch.

```
8:30 P.M.  (1 bell)   Clang
9:00 P.M.  (2 bells)  Clang-clang.
9:30 P.M.  (3 bells)  Clang-clang, clang
10:00 P.M. (4 bells)  Clang-clang, clang-clang.
10:30 P.M. (5 bells)  Clang-clang, clang-clang, clang,
11:00 P.M. (6 bells)  Clang-clang, clang-clang, clang-clang.
11:30 P.M. (7 bells)  Clang-clang, clang-clang, clang-clang, clang.
12:00 P.M. (8 bells)  Clang-clang, clang-clang, clang-clang, clang-clang.
```

THOSE NEVER-ENDING DECK CHORES!

Sleek hull, soaring masts, countless ropes that must mean something to someone, glistening brasswork, polished teak deck houses and smooth, spotless decks, freshly-tarred standing rigging that stood out against the painted yards and masts - the tall ship would excite the imagination of any would-be sailor. This graceful, crisply maintained lady of the seas owed her sparkle to the seamen who called her home. Their calloused hands, blistered fingers, nails with tell-tale traces of tar, patches on the knees of pants flecked with paint were proof enough of the considerable energies that must be expended to keep this lady tidy and respectable. As they would tell you, "She is like a lady's watch, always out of repair!"

Work aboard had two extremes ~ and neither was easy. The first ~ putting one's seamanship skills into practice ~ was a source of pride for any professional seagoer. He was sure-footed on the ratlines, could furl a sail before a squall struck, measure the ship's speed with the log, sound depths with the lead, anticipate shifting winds and seas while at the helm, and could tie the right knot at the right time and place. And then there was the pure and simple drudgery of endless repair and maintenance. This was the less glamorous side of sea life, and it deserves a closer look.

Deck work had a rhythm about it, however boring. Getting underway called for seeing to any rigging stress, checking the new canvas for the rounding of Cape Horn, securing the cargo and hatches against rough weather, and like preparations. The Calms of the Atlantic and Pacific Horse Latitudes and the Doldrums were right for deck sanding, painting, and tarring. While the Cape itself kept the crewmen busy at the helm, managing the rigging and sails or just hanging on, the passage home was spent sprucing up the square-rigger. The owners would be waiting on the dock, and anything less than a ship-shape appearance just wouldn't do.

SWABBING THE DECKS ~
Wooden decks were washed and scrubbed daily. Not only was the bare wood kept bright and clean, but the moistened planks would not shrink and open at the seams.

Sea water must be hoisted aboard for the swabbing. At the waist of the ship, a spar was lashed so that it extended a few feet outboard. At its end was a block, and through it was rove a rope attached to a large canvas bucket. A seaman stood on the pinrail and swung the bucket forward. By the time it filled, it had drifted under the spar. Two men bent their backs to pull in the bucket rope. Once hoisted to deck height, it was tipped into a large wooden tub. When the tub was filled, smaller buckets were dipped in and then passed down a line of crewmen to the mate. He

"PRAYER-BOOK," A SMALL HOLYSTONE, WAS SCRUBBED WITH WHILE THE SAILOR WAS ON HIS KNEES. THE NAME WAS APPROPRIATE.

would then slosh the contents in front of four seamen armed with brooms. Bare-footed and pants rolled up, they scrubbed as fast as they could to keep up with the tireless mate and his constant call for more buckets of water.

SANDING THE DECK ~
Occasionally, when seas permitted, the deck was holystoned. After the deck was wet down, beach sand was sprinkled over the entire surface. This was one of the few deck chores that were made easier in rainy weather, otherwise sea water must be hauled up over the side. The holystone,

c. 1870 ~ 1920

CANVAS DRAW BUCKETS FOR LIFTING SEA WATER ABOARD. THE ONE ON THE RIGHT IS ON THE HALF-MODEL SHIP "LAGODA," NEW BEDFORD WHALING MUSEUM (THE ASHLEY BOOK OF KNOTS.)

a large soft stone with a smooth underside, was used to scrub the wet sand over the deck under pressure. This was done by sliding the stone fore and aft (the lay of the planking) by means of long ropes attached to the ends. Usually the sanding process began at the poop deck aft and worked toward the bow.

Smaller hand stones, called by the sailors "prayer-book," were used on the hands and knees to renew the deck surfaces too small for the holystone. To be thorough, even the steps of the forecastle and hatchways were hauled up to be cleaned off with "prayer-books" and wet sand. When smooth and white, the deck was washed free of sand and dried off with swabs.

c.1840~1880
DECK BUCKET.

BUCKET RAIL AND WOODEN BUCKETS FOR CARRYING WATER. BOTH WERE USUALLY OF TEAK, AND THE BUCKETS WERE BOUND WITH BRASS OR IRON STRAPS. HOUSED AT THE BREAK OF THE POOP~ THE AFTERMOST DECK.

c.1800-1880
KIT = A DECK BUCKET LARGER AT THE BOTTOM. AND LESS APT TO CAPSIZE.

Sanding the teakwood rail moldings, doors, and deckhouses was a tedious chore at best. It took days to free the old varnish with sand and a folded piece of canvas. It was considered a proper job for the apprentices. The use of knives and scrapers was forbidden, even though they could do the job in several hours. Officers were conscious of the old proverb that "The Devil soon finds mischief for idle hands to do." It would seem that the Devil would have slim pickings on the old square-riggers.

POLISHING ~ Tarnished brasswork "reflected" badly on any ship. Bright and sparkling it must be, and that included the capstan trim, ship's bells, and bucket and harness cask strappings.

PAINTING ~ Rust ~ that arch-enemy of the iron-hulled tall ship ~ and loose paint must be scraped and sanded whenever sea conditions permitted. Once in the trade winds, it was safe enough to lower a stage over the side of the ship. The fresh coat went on right to the water line. With little rolling of the hull, the sail-supporting ropes might be loosened so that the yards could be painted. Masts should be freshened as well, but woe be to the poor soul who dribbled on the deck from aloft!

TARRING ~ For the standing rigging, this was a must every six months on a long voyage. With the entire crew "pitching" in, the job could be done in a single day. Tarring began at the masthead rigging ~ its loftiest point of attachment ~ and worked downward. When the level of a yardarm was reached, the tarring of the lifts and footropes would start at the ends and work toward the mast.

By far the most difficult part of this weatherproofing was the backstays (the high

$\frac{1}{3}$ x

c.1800-1860

HULL SCRAPER
(FORT TICONDEROGA, NEW YORK.)

"RIDING DOWN" THE BACKSTAYS.

A SAFETY LINE SHOULD CONNECT THE SAILOR'S BELT TO THE STAY. THIS "STEEPLE-JACK KNOT" WILL EASILY SLIP UP OR DOWN WITH HAND PRESSURE. IF HE FALLS, THE KNOT WILL NOT SLIP WHEN HIS WEIGHT FALLS ON IT.

THIS BOATSWAIN'S CHAIR IS SECURED WITH A BOWLINE KNOT.

standing rigging that supported both sides of the mast). A long rope was rove through a single block where the stays attached to the mast. At its end, a bow-line secured the boatswain's chair—it was little more than a child's swing. The deck end was lashed and eased off gradually as the tarring continued. "Holydays"—spots that were missed—were not tolerated, and Jack would find himself aloft once again if the tarring was less than perfect. It was a dangerous business, with nothing below but air, a hard deck or the sea.

CATCHING RAIN WATER ~ Fresh water at sea was a luxury whenever the heavens opened up to deliver this liquid treasure. It must be caught and preserved for drier spells. The "harness-cask"~that large wooden tub that was used for soaking out the salt in preserved meat~was scrubbed out and then hauled to the aft cabin. Its roof acted as a sort of basin, and from it the rain water was funneled off and down a short tube to the cask. Deck buckets were filled from this reservoir and carried to the empty water casks on deck.

Oil skins or not, the sailors on watch duty would be drenched to the hide in the pelting rain. Spillage when pouring the water into the copper bung-hole funnel didn't help. Since the first catch was usually brackish, it might be used for scrubbing panelwork with sand and canvas.

Certainly idleness was hard to come by. Minor chores, less than inspiring, seemed never-ending. For example, the "head" (latrine) must be scrubbed, coal fetched for the cook, and the ship's lamps filled and trimmed. There was always a need for oakum. Used for caulking, it was made by picking apart old rope into its fibers. Some mates placed coils of tired roping about the ships as oakum stations for any empty hands. Twisted into a loose yarn, the oakum was tarred before caulking. Finally, if a watch seemed to be easing off, the anchor and its chains were available for scraping. As the old saying went,

"Six days shalt thou labor and do all thou art able,
And on the seventh ~ holystone the decks and scrape the cable."

KNOTTY BUT NICE

The versatile bowline, used on the boatswain's chair, could be a lifesaver. It was one of countless knots used for deck work on all rope-rigged sailing ships. More than that, it was one of the deepwater sailor's most cherished arts, and there was an abundance of weathered and condemned rope for plenty of practice. The most lubberly newcomer aboard would be well advised to keep his eyes peeled and ears uncorked when the crew gathered in the forecastle to match their skills. Some day he would be tying his own beckets (rope handles) for his sea chest and ditty bag lanyards. Such fancy knots were the owner's pride and envy of his ship-mates.

But one must float before he can swim. There were the basic everyday knots that were vital to the business of sailing, and master them one must before trying one's hand with those not only useful but ornamental. To become an ordinary seaman, or for today's sail trainees to be part of the team effort, the language of knot tying and tying the knot itself should be second nature.

Clifford Ashley, the dean of all knotting artists, said this about knot terminology ~

"A splice is PUT IN, a hitch is MADE FAST or TAKEN, two ropes are BENT together, a knot is PUT IN, MADE or CAST in a rope. A sailor TAKES A TURN, he BELAYS; he CLAPS ON a stopper, he SLACKS AWAY, and CASTS OFF a line. He CLEARS a tangle, he OPENS a jammed knot, and he WORKS a Turk's-Head or a sennit. The word TIE is used so seldom by the sailor only because it is too general a term for daily use, where something specific is almost always called for. But when a sailor refers to the subject as a whole he always speaks of 'tying knots' or 'knot tying.'"

Knots are known by their function. At sea, they are known by four classifications ~ hitches, bends, knots, and splices.

1. A HITCH makes a rope fast to another object.

~ TWO HALF HITCHES ~

THE MOST USED FOR HITCHING
TO MOORINGS AND FOR GENERAL UTILITY.

~ THE ROLLING HITCH ~
BEST FOR BENDING A
SMALL ROPE TO A
LARGER TAUT ROPE.

ONE OF THE MOST
FREQUENTLY USED
KNOTS ON SHIPBOARD.

THE TIMBER HITCH WAS MUCH USED FOR HAULING CARGO, SPARS, AND SMALL CRATES.

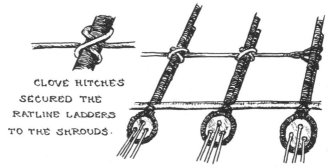

CLOVE HITCHES SECURED THE RATLINE LADDERS TO THE SHROUDS.

2. A BEND unites two rope ends.

~THE SHEET BEND~

THE SHEET ROPES RAN THROUGH EACH YARDARM AND WERE USED FOR SETTING THE SAIL. THIS BEND WAS THE TIE USED AND REMAINS THE PREFERRED BEND ABOARD SHIP.

3. A KNOT was a knob, loop, and anything not included under hitches, bends, and splices. Fancy and trick knots are Represented here.

~THE SQUARE KNOT ~ ALSO KNOWN AS A REEF KNOT, WAS ONE OF THE BEST BINDING KNOTS GOING, IT WAS USED TO REEF AND FURL SAILS AND TO TIE PACKAGES. IT MUST NEVER BE USED AS A BEND, FOR TWO ROPES JOINED TOGETHER IN A SQUARE KNOT WOULD SURELY SLIP IF JERKED. THERE WERE MORE DEATHS FROM ITS MISUSE THAN ALL OTHER KNOTS COMBINED!

THE SQUARE-KNOTTED NECKERCHIEF. (SEE "DECKING OUT THE SEAMAN.")

THE BOWLINE KNOT NAME WAS DERIVED FROM THE BOW LINE THAT HELD THE SIDE OF A SAIL FORWARD TO PREVENT THE SAILS FROM BEING TAKEN ABACK (IF WIND SUDDENLY BLOWS ON THE FRONT OF THE SAILS INSTEAD OF BEHIND). THAT USE IS NOW OBSOLETE, BUT IT IS THE USUAL LOOP KNOT FOR TYING A BOAT TO A RING, AS A "MONKEY ROPE" FOR LOWERING A MAN OVER THE SIDE, AND FOR MOORING TO POSTS.

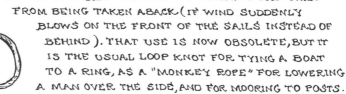

4. A SPLICE joins two rope ends by interweaving the strands. Ropes woven together would include running rigging, cargo, and deck gear. A marlinespike may help open the strands.

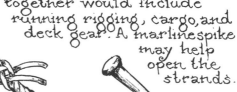

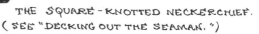

THE " SHORT" SPLICE.

WHERE ARE WE?

While the seamen were scrambling up the ratlines or keeping the ship in decent repair, the officers looked to their navigational instruments. To these must be added a generous amount of not-so-common sea sense to reach safe harbor. The ship's location in the vastness of the ocean depended on it, and if no one aboard knew where he'd been or where he was, he would certainly be "all at sea" as to where he was going.

THE ART OF NAVIGATION

The first mate gathered all the facts he could and recorded them daily in the ship's logbook. It was a sort of diary about the daily happenings aboard, sea conditions, ocean bottom, soundings, wind and weather, the number of sails set, ocean currents, courses, and speed being made. From this information he estimated the ship's position. In the seventeenth and eighteenth centuries, this educated guess was known as "deduced reckoning" but was abbreviated to "ded reckoning" to save logbook space. Pronounced "dead reckoning" this theoretical location of the ship (for there were no convenient signposts or landfalls to sight on the high seas) was plotted on the chart to show the distance believed to have been covered along each course steered.

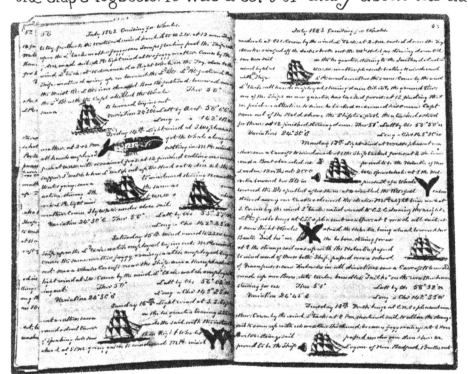

A "SPOUTERS" LOGBOOK DRAWINGS AND INKED STAMPS ILLUSTRATED SIGHTINGS AND UNUSUAL HAPPENINGS. HORIZONTAL WHALES INDICATED THOSE SIGHTED BUT NOT CAPTURED. A VERTICAL WHALE WOULD SHOW ONE HAULED ABOARD AFTER SECTIONING.

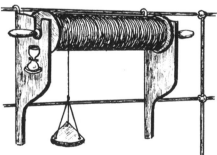

LOG LINE AND LOG "CHIP" WITH REEL, STORED ON AFT RAILING.

SHIP'S SPEED ~ The log "chip" measured the ship's speed—not distance—and has been in use since the English thought it up back in the late fifteenth century. Since the rate of progress varied throughout the sea day, each watch recorded its log findings for later plotting. The log "chip" itself was a triangular piece of wood, weighted with lead at its curved base so that it would float upright in the water. Attached to the log (it WAS a chunk of log in earlier days) was the log line, knotted at intervals to represent a fraction of the nautical mile. It was payed out from a log reel for half a minute before recording.

While one seaman held the reel over his head, a companion heaved the log "chip" over the stern. The log "chip" remained stationary in the water, and as the ship moved ahead, the long line

AS SHIP MOVES FORWARD, THE KNOTTED
LOG LINE UNREELS.

START TIMING WHEN WHITE CLOTH MARK REACHES
TAFFRAIL AND LOG "CHIP" BEYOND WAKE.

LINE REELED, AND PLUG
PULLS OUT TO FLOAT LOG "CHIP."

LOG "CHIP" WITH LEAD-
WEIGHTED EDGE. THE PLUG
DISLODGES WHEN LOG LINE
STOPS RUNNING OUT.

CAPSIZED 30-SECOND
SAND GLASS.

began to unreel. A piece of white bunting was tied to the line, and when this was seen passing over the stern rail, the log was well beyond the ship's wake and dead in the water. This small white flag signaled the beginning of the measured knots, and the sailor holding the reel shouted "Turn!" A "boy," holding a thirty-second sand glass, turned it over to start the timing. When it emptied, he yelled "Stop!" The line was seized to prevent any further paying out, and at that point the ship began to tow the log. The forward pressure yanked out a wooden plug that was wedged into one of the log's three corners. The two lines to the remaining corners floated the log, and it was hauled aboard.

When the number of knots was counted (each $\frac{1}{120}$th of a nautical mile apart), the speed could be recorded by multiplying that number by 120 ~ the number of half minutes in an hour. This gave the number of knots per hour. Since a nautical mile is 6080 feet (instead of the 5280 feet on land), a ship sailing at three knots would be going at 3 nautical miles (18,240 feet) per hour.

MECHANICAL LOGS ~ many mechanical logs were developed, but it wasn't until the 1850s that they were perfected for general use. The "harpoon" log of the 1860s combined rotating blades with recording dials to indicate the rate of speed.

THE "HARPOON" LOG WITH SPEED DIALS.
(PEABODY MUSEUM OF SALEM.)

The Walker Company's "Cherub" log of 1879 had both a flywheel and propeller, was attached to a torque-free line, and had a convenient counter mounted on the ship's rail. One of its claims to fame was that it repelled those large fish that had thought earlier logs were lunch. Although the French invented the first electric log in 1902, it was not until 1924 that the entire log could reliably send the ratio of the fin or wheel rotations to the counter inboard. The log could then remain in the water without being hauled in for recording.

THE CHERNIKEEFF LOG HAS A SMALL
FAN IN THE TUBE THAT EXTENDS TO
THE SHIP'S BOTTOM. THE ROTATIONS
ARE ELECTRICALLY REGISTERED ON BOARD.

COMPASS ~ Although the speed in knots per hour was known, the wind-jammer rarely sailed a straight course. Coming about frequently on different tacks gave a zig-zag passage that must be reckoned. Each new direction was recorded in the logbook from the compass readings along with the time of change.

When determining the ship's position, the compass was the navigator's best friend, but like most friends, it must be understood to be appreciated.

COMPASS RIM.

THICK GLASS COVER.

RUBBER GASKET PREVENTS LEAKAGE AND EVAPORATION OF THE BOWL'S LIQUID.

THE COMPASS CARD IS MARKED WITH DIRECTIONAL POINTS AND DEGREES. MAGNETIZED NEEDLES ARE ATTACHED TO THE UNDERSIDE OF THE CARD AND LINE UP WITH THE WORLD'S NORTH AND SOUTH MAGNETIC POLES. THE CARD'S NORTH POINTS TO MAGNETIC NORTH ~ NOT THE TRUE NORTH POLE.

THE MARINER'S COMPASS IS A "WET" COMPASS AND IS FILLED WITH WATER AND ALCOHOL OR GLYCERINE TO PREVENT FREEZING. THE LIQUID FLOATS THE COMPASS CARD AND SLOWS OR DAMPENS THE SIDE-TO-SIDE SWING OF THE CARD FROM THE SHIP'S MOTION.

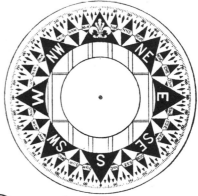

COMPASS CARD.

THE LUBBER'S LINE POINTS TO THE BOW AND SHOWS THE COMPASS DIRECTION IN WHICH THE SHIP IS HEADING.

THE COMPASS CARD RESTS ON A PIVOT TO PERMIT A FREE ROTATION.

GIMBALS KEEP THE BOWL LEVEL WHILE THE SHIP PITCHES AND ROLLS.

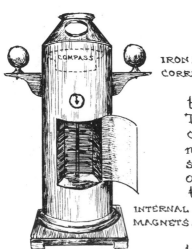

COMPASS

IRON BALL CORRECTORS.

INTERNAL MAGNETS.

BINNACLE.

DEVIATION ERRORS ~ That best friend of the navigator, the compass, had its share of problems as most friends do. There are countless iron or steel objects aboard ~ particularly on a steel-hulled sailer ~ that would attract the magnet and give false readings. These deviations are corrected with a compass housing called a binnacle (from the early English word "bitakle" meaning "little house"). Internal magnets and the two soft iron "corrector" balls cancel out the magnetic attraction of the ship's ironwear and must be done before taking to the sea lanes.

VARIATION ERRORS ~ Since the magnetic north pole is located slightly to the north of Hudson's Bay and not at the true north pole of the earth, the compass rarely points to the

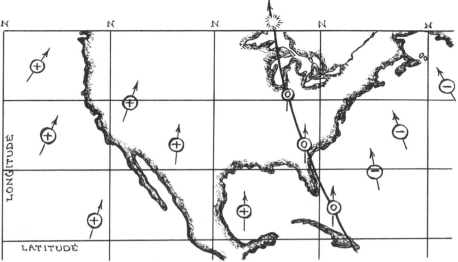

N = TRUE NORTH.   ☀ = MAGNETIC NORTH.   ——— 0° VARIATION.
VARIATION IS THE DIFFERENCE BETWEEN TRUE AND MAGNETIC
NORTH.   ⊕→ = ADD THE DIFFERENCE TO FIND TRUE NORTH.
⊖→ = SUBTRACT THE DIFFERENCE IN DEGREES.

magnetic and the earth's poles at the same time. Therefore, this difference or "variation" of degrees is added or subtracted after referring to a declination chart. The true course, based on true north, may then be plotted on the chart.

THE GYROCOMPASS

By 1910, the gyrocompass had revolutionized navigation. Its heart was the gyroscope ~ basically a spinning wheel on an axis that always rotated in the same plane, regardless of the ship's course, pitch, or roll. Once aimed at true north it would always point in that direction, uninfluenced by magnetic fields and without the errors of deviation or variation. Here was a navigator's dream come true!

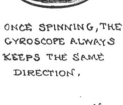

The gyroscope has two basic forces. Gyroscopic INERTIA keeps the axis of the spinning wheel (rotor) pointing in the same direction, regardless of how the base is tilted. If a child rolls a hoop, its axis will remain parallel to the ground and on a straight course. When the spinning hoop slows or stops, the wheel has lost its inertia and falls over. The gyrocompass uses this force to point the compass needle directly toward true north.

ONCE SPINNING, THE
GYROSCOPE ALWAYS
KEEPS THE SAME
DIRECTION.

A second force is PRECESSION. When the hoop is pushed from the side, it tends to move in a right angle to that pressure. Gravity exerts such a pressure ~ unless the rotor is horizontal ~ as when the axis is tilted toward true north. As the earth revolves, the axis turns over to keep in line with true north. To correct this gravitational turning effect, a hollow "U" tube filled with mercury is attached to the inner gimbal. The mercury flows freely to seek its lowest level and keeps the axis in a horizontal position. The gyroscope no longer twists as the earth turns, and it remains in line with the earth's surface meridians (great imaginary circles that connect both north and south poles).

INNER GIMBAL.

GRAVITY.

DIRECTION IS MAINTAINED
IN SPITE OF TILTING.

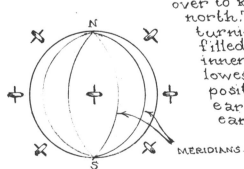

MERIDIANS.

WITH THE PRECESSION FORCE CORRECTED, THE AXIS DOES NOT DIP
DIRECTLY AT NORTH BUT RATHER STAYS PARALLEL TO THE MERIDIANS.

The gyrocompass was available to many of our naval craft in time for World War I. It would be a rare large ship today that did not take advantage of this accurate indicator of true north. The average gyrocompass has a rotor of about eleven inches across and weighs fifty-five pounds. A motor drives the rotor at 6000 revolutions per minute. But this is no time to ignore the time-honored magnetic compass. Only the largest of the square-riggers use the gyrocompass, for its size, cost, and complicated construction that needs an expert for repairs make it less practical for smaller sailers. Even with the gyrocompass aboard, the magnetic compass is also there as a backup and to check gyrocompass accuracy.

COMPASS CARD

LUBBER RING

SPEED AND LATITUDE CORRECTOR

SPIDER ELEMENT

CARDAN RING

BINNACLE RING

ROLL DAMPER

AZIMUTH MOTOR

PITCH DAMPER

HEADING TRANSMITTER

WIRE SUSPENSION

ROTOR AND CASE

PHANTOM ELEMENT

MERCURY BALLISTIC

SPINNING AXIS

VERTICAL RING

VERTICAL AXIS
φ

HORIZONTAL AXIS

THE GYROCOMPASS IN SCHEMATIC DETAIL.
(THE SPERRY GYROSCOPE COMPANY)

MORE ON DEAD RECKONING ~

The first mate now had the speed of the ship and the length of time on each tack to determine the distance sailed. He had recorded the courses steered from corrected compass readings. He therefore had at hand the most important information needed to chart his estimated position ~ his deduced reckoning. But before he took his parallel ruler and dividers in hand, he would consider a few lesser variables.

LEEWAY DRIFT ~

There was a possibility of the ship drifting sideways as she continued her course. This was certainly so when the wind was well forward of the ship's beam ~ the widest part of the ship ① and especially when the wind blew broadside ②. Heavy seas could slow the vessel and increase the leeway (the lee is the side away from the wind). If the wind were abaft the beam, the lee drift would be much less ③ and if it were directly astern, there would be no drift at all ④.

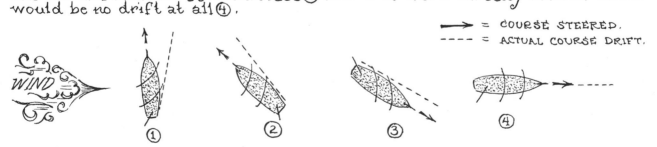

⟶ = COURSE STEERED.
---- = ACTUAL COURSE DRIFT.

WIND

①　②　③　④

Since wind leeway offers no precise measurements, the experienced mate would add his educated guess to the deduced reckoning position.

CURRENT DRIFT ~

Current charts are available in the "Pilot Charts." Their influence on the ship's position would be estimated and calculated into the plotting of her present whereabouts.

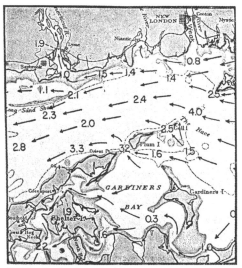

TIDAL CURRENT CHART WITH THE DIRECTION
AND SPEED IN KNOTS OF CURRENTS.

SOUNDINGS~ If the navigator had his choice of only two instruments, the compass would be the first, and the lead line for measuring depths would run a close second. For a more accurate D.R ~ the deduced reckoning position-periodic soundings of the sea bottom were a real help. This is particulary true in shoal waters, and the only safe guide when socked in by fog or in narrow passages, and when measuring the varied depths of high and low tide. A ship, wedged high and dry on a sand bar in shallows, is certainly a danger and an embarrassment no one can afford.

The character of the sea bottom may be determined by arming the hollow of the lead base with tallow or grease. The sand, mud, shells, and pebbles give information on the ship's location.

Usually a lead weighed seven or fourteen pounds with ten to twenty fathoms of line. A twenty-five-pound lead with one hundred fathoms of line was useful in heavy weather or for deep seas (the "dipsey" lead). When the ship was underway, the leadsman stood in the "chains"~ a platform that projected from the ship's side and secured by chains as well as deadeyes from the lower standing rigging. The lead was heaved forward. As the ship moved ahead, the line became perpendicular, and the line's markings at the ocean surface indicated the depth. "Marks" on the line represented fathoms~ a fathom equals six feet.

FATHOMS
- 2 = Two strips of leather.
- 3 = Three strips of leather.
- 5 = White cotton rag.
- 7 = Red woolen bunting.
- 10 = Piece of leather with a hole in it.
- 13 = Same as 3.
- 15 = Same as 5.
- 17 = Same as 7.
- 20 = Cord with two knots.
- 25 = Cord with one knot.
- 30 = Cord with three knots.

"HEAVING THE LEAD." THREE OR FOUR SWINGS OVER THE HEAD GAVE GREATER DISTANCE.

(WILBUR- PIRATES AND PATRIOTS OF THE REVOLUTION).

Estimated fathoms between the fathom marks are called "deeps." With each heave of the lead, the leadsman would sing out readings that would sound like this: "By the mark two!" (formerly "mark twain!") is a two-fathom sounding~ "And a quarter five!" is five-and-a-quarter fathoms~ "And a half five!" is five-and-a-half fathoms~ "Quarter less five!" is four-and-three-fourths of a fathom~ "By the deep four!" is an estimated four fathoms between the three and five fathom marks~ "No bottom at twenty!" speaks for itself.

THE FATHOMETER~ This modern "echo sounder" is now used by most classes of larger sailers. In the bottom of the hull, an oscillator pulses down a sound of such intensity that it bounces off the ocean floor and back to a receiver. The time difference between sending the sound and receiving the echo indicates the depth. A fathometer dial will show this in fathoms. But when the ship is in less than fifteen fathoms of water, the old reliable lead line is broken out and put to work.

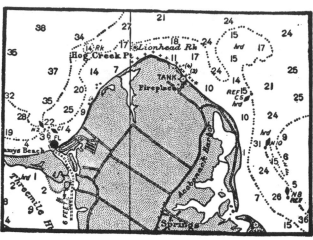

CHART SHOWING DEPTHS IN FEET. THREE AND FIVE FATHOM UNITS ARE SHOWN IN DOTTED LINES.

THE MERCATOR CHART

With distance, course, depth, and character of the ocean bottom, leeway drift and currents estimated as best he could, the first mate set about plotting the ship's position. The tools were modest enough~ a pair of parallel rulers, a pair of dividers, a navigational table book, a nautical almanac and a series of charts (charts, not maps!) of the seas to be sailed.

Navigational charts are Mercator charts~ a flattened version of the earth's sphere.

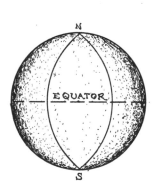

MERIDIAN CUTS RUN FROM POLE TO POLE.

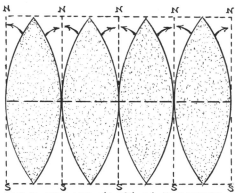

THE FLATTENED GLOBE IS EXPANDED FROM POLE TO EQUATOR INTO STRAIGHT VERTICAL LINES (LONGITUDES).

LONGITUDE ~ If a series of cuts were made on an orange from top to bottom, pole to pole, they would represent the globe's meridians. They would be perpendicular to a great circle, the equator, around the earth midway between the north and south poles.

Now if the orange skin were to be flattened, the curved meridians must be straightened into vertical parallel north and south lines, still perpendicular to the equator. Obviously, the farther away from the equator, the more distorted and broader than normal are land masses and east and west distances. But at least each meridian runs true north and south, and this makes plotting a chart possible.

The meridian that passes through Greenwich, England is arbitrarily considered the prime or 0° meridian. Meridians run both to the east and to the west to 180° ~ halfway around the earth where east meets west (circumference = 360°). These are the LONGITUDES ~ defined

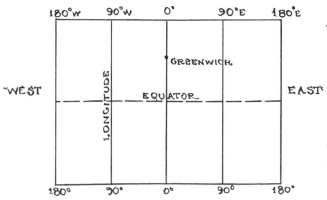

as a position on the earth east or west from the meridian of Greenwich, and recorded on a chart as 0°–180°E or 0°–180°W.

LATITUDE is the measurement of one's distance on the earth north or south of the equator. Each "parallel" of latitude is represented on the chart as a horozontal straight line. Latitude is measured from 0° on the equator, north or south to 90° at either pole.

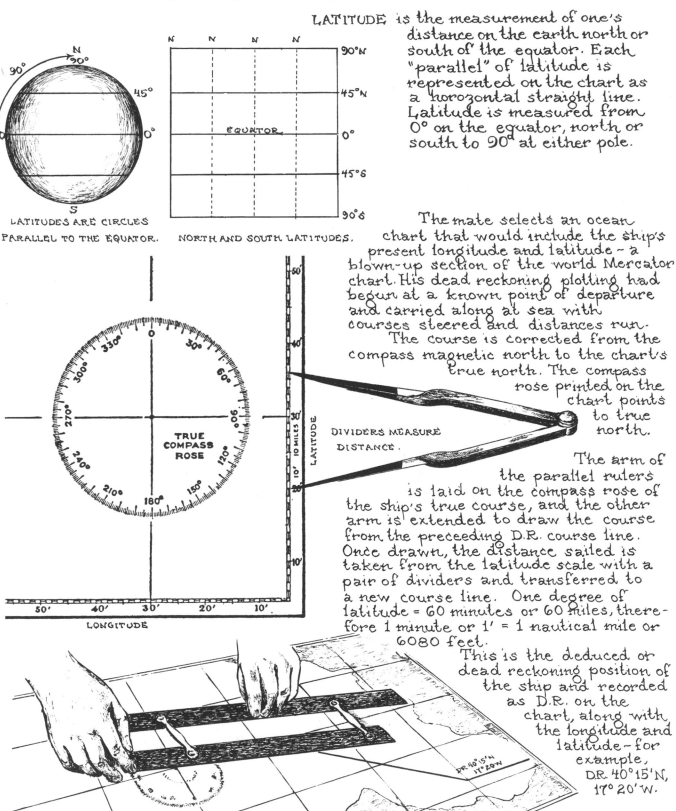

LATITUDES ARE CIRCLES PARALLEL TO THE EQUATOR.

NORTH AND SOUTH LATITUDES.

TRUE COMPASS ROSE

DIVIDERS MEASURE DISTANCE.

LONGITUDE

The mate selects an ocean chart that would include the ship's present longitude and latitude – a blown-up section of the world Mercator chart. His dead reckoning plotting had begun at a known point of departure and carried along at sea with courses steered and distances run.

The course is corrected from the compass magnetic north to the chart's true north. The compass rose printed on the chart points to true north.

The arm of the parallel rulers is laid on the compass rose of the ship's true course, and the other arm is extended to draw the course from the preceeding D.R. course line. Once drawn, the distance sailed is taken from the latitude scale with a pair of dividers and transferred to a new course line. One degree of latitude = 60 minutes or 60 miles, therefore 1 minute or 1' = 1 nautical mile or 6080 feet.

This is the deduced or dead reckoning position of the ship and recorded as D.R. on the chart, along with the longitude and latitude – for example, D.R. 40°15'N, 17° 20' W.

The true and magnetic compass rose is printed on enlarged coastal charts. As with the true compass rose on deep-water charts, true north is in line with the longitudes. Coastal charts include an imprint of the magnetic degrees and the variation error for each offshore locality. Since short runs are the rule, the magnetic rose is easier to use from direct magnetic compass readings. The course would not differ greatly from the true course. This would never do on the high seas, where long courses would compound the variation error.

THE CELESTIAL FIX

With the sextant and the chronometer, the captain determines the position at sea independently of the mate's deduced reckoning. His measurements of latitude and longitude will "fix" the ship's location and be used as a cross-check of the mate's estimated course.

LATITUDE ~ Each noon, the sun is over the same meridian as that of the ship. The height of the sun is constant for midday, depending on the day, month, and year. The sextant measures this height by finding the angle formed by sighting the lowest part of the sun and the horizon. The nearer the latitude to the equator, the greater the angle. This noon sextant angle reading is then matched to the navigational tables in a nautical almanac for that time and date.

THE SEXTANT MEASURES THE ANGLE BETWEEN THE SUN OR STAR AND THE SEA HORIZON TO CALCULATE THE SHIP'S LATITUDE.

THE SEXTANT

~PARTS OF A SEXTANT~
1. INDEX MIRROR REFLECTS THE SUN TO THE HORIZON GLASS, MOVES WITH THE ARM.
2. HORIZON GLASS ~ CLEAR AND IMMOVABLE.
3. SHADES SWING DOWN WHEN VIEWING THE SUN.
4. TELESCOPE DIRECTS LINE OF SIGHT AND MAGNIFIES.
5. VIEW THROUGH THE TELESCOPE. LOWER EDGE OF SUN'S IMAGE IS BROUGHT TO THE HORIZON.
6. ARM IS MOVED TO LINE UP SUN TO THE HORIZON.
7. ARC WITH DEGREES OF THE ANGLE OF SUN TO THE HORIZON.
8. INDEX ~ DEGREE READING IS RECORDED AT THE ARROW.

THE LONGITUDE is the ship's position east or west of the Greenwich meridian ~ where high noon is 0°. At sea, when the sextant sightings show the exact moment that it enters the ship's meridian ~ its maximum altitude above the ship ~ the chronometer's Greenwich time is read. For example, if the chronometer says 2:30, the ship is 2½ hours east or west of Greenwich. Since the earth revolves 360° every 24 hours, it must turn 15° every hour. In 2½ hours the earth will have turned 37° and 30 minutes east or west longitude. When the longitude and latitude are charted, the intersecting lines give a fix for the ship's position.

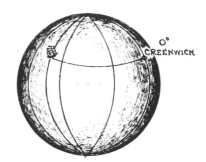

TIME DEGREE DIFFERENCE FROM 0° IS SHIP'S LONGITUDE.

The chronometer, perfected in the 1820s, keeps the time of Greenwich, England, with extreme accuracy. The time keeper rests on two sets of gimbals to keep level despite the ship's movement. A glass lid protects the mechanism from moisture and temperature and is raised for winding.

THE CHRONOMETER.

PILOTING

SECOND BEARING.   FIRST BEARING.

Navigation, then, is finding one's position when out of sight of land. Piloting, on the other hand, is finding one's location in sight of land. The usual way to "get one's bearings" is to sight known landmarks with the pelorus. Because it is not magnetized, it is known as a "dumb" compass.

The north on the pelorus card is first lined up to the magnetic compass north. The vanes are then turned until the landmark is sighted. The bearing is read on the card beneath the far vane. If another known object is sighted at the same time, the two bearings are plotted to find the exact location of the ship.

WIND AND WEATHER

AIR PRESSURE~ Any arthritic sailor will tell you that he can expect foul weather when his joints act up. His bodily cells now have relatively less pressure than that of the atmosphere, and the gases in his joint cells expanded outward to cause aching in his sensitive joints. True enough, but the pressure changes of a barometer will give a more accurate picture of changing weather conditions. A rapidly falling pressure confirms that a storm is just over the horizon. A rising barometer tells of good weather ahead.

COLD AIR   WARM AIR

Although the mercury barometer is a tad more accurate, the liquid-free aneroid barometer will show much slighter pressure changes and is easily carried on shipboard. Its workings consist of a metal vacuum box that expands or contracts with the air pressure upon it. A long pointer on the barometer face moves with any pressure variation. The shorter pointer is first set by hand on the reading of the long pointer. When read again, the long pointer will have risen or fallen. The more rapid the change, the sooner the weather shift.

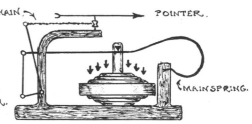

CHAIN   POINTER.

MAINSPRING.

INSIDE THE ANEROID BAROMETER.

WIND is the movement of air as it warms or cools. A stove will warm the air above it, which rises as the molecules expand. Cold air pushes in to replace it and in turn is heated and moves upward. A current of air is now circulating from ceiling to floor, much like "Predicting The Wind's Direction," on an earlier page and on a grander scale. When cold and heavier polar air masses meet moist tropical air, changes in pressure, wind, temperature and humidity will follow.

Since wind makes waves, it follows that the greater the wind, the larger the waves. Fresh breezes may build seas of ten or more feet, and heavier winds may create giants of fifty feet or more. Officially, a fifty-mile-an-hour wind is rated as a "strong gale" and will undoubtedly cause some damage to the tall ship before the blow is over.

When running before a strong wind in heavy seas, one of the helmsman's most terrifying experiences is to see huge waves building up and towering over the stern. In earlier days, the helmsman might be lashed to the wheel on the poop deck so that he wouldn't be washed overboard—or to prevent his leaving the wheel for safer quarters. Today, most large steel full-riggers and barks have a curved steel

POOP DECK HOUSING FOR THE HELMSMAN'S SURVIVAL.

housing around the steering wheel to prevent just such a disaster. If you've ever been "pooped," perhaps you are comparing yourself to the exhausted helmsman on the poop—the after deck.

As for gales, the violence of a Cape Horn "snorter" can only be imagined when the gusts last for weeks and the course is westerly "into the teeth of the wind." Old salts talk of a gale at its height as "blowing like scissors and thumb-screws." Captain Irving Johnson rounded the Cape on the "Peking" (now in safe harbor at New York's South Street Seaport) in 1929. He told me of gales that pounded the ship with 150-mile-an-hour winds. Its unearthly screeching was so loud that if a sailor hollered, he couldn't hear himself! The mast tops were swinging in arcs of over three hundred feet, and many of these rolls angled to 45° in a short eleven seconds.

BUOY

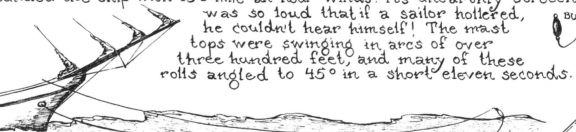

THE FLOATING ANCHOR, USED TO RIDE OUT A GALE.
THE SHIP HAS TAKEN IN CANVAS AND RIDES WITH BARE POLES.
(SEAMANSHIP, 1811)

CANVAS SEWN TO IRON FRAME.

The decks were constantly awash, and little remained dry below. The "Peking" shrieked and groaned as if in pain and shuddered as though it would be her last moment afloat.

Indeed, Cape Horn seemed to be the devil's own storehouse for miserable weather. This was particularly true when the ship was making westward passage and sailing into the headwinds of the "Roaring Forties." Almost a century earlier than the "Peking's" passage, Richard Dana faced the same predicament.

There was a constant cry of "Ice ahead!"—"Ice on the lee bow!"~"Another island!" And there were gale winds and sleet (snow was called "Cape Horn sugar") enough to keep the lookout edgy. Foul weather or not, Dana and his mates were frequently aloft. He recalled "...that the yardarm over which we lay was cased in ice, the gaskets and rope of the foot and leach of each sail as stiff and hard as a piece of suction-hose, and the sail itself about as pliable as though it had been made of sheathing copper nailed together." Mittens had no place at such frozen heights, for if the sailor slipped, it would be his last misadventure. "We had need of every finger God had given us." He and the crew beat their hands upon the sail to keep them from freezing.

Perhaps this is the proper time to mention two golden rules of sailing—
1. Never go aloft on the lee rigging. Always go aloft to the windward, then cross over to the leeward when you get as high as you want to go.
2. When aloft, never let go of a rope until you have a grip on another, or~ one hand for the ship, and one for yourself.

Drenching gales called for "soul and body lashings"—rope yarn about the legs and wrists of the sailor's oilskins. Another length was wrapped around the waist to prevent the oilskin jacket from being blown over the head. Sometimes it was an exercise in futility, for heavy rains seemed to trickle under the lashings on their way to soaking the seaman's hide ~ yet had some trouble draining under and away from those same rope ties.

FOG ~ Warm air, saturated with moisture, condenses as it contacts cooler air. The temperature must drop below the dew point for the pea soup effect.
With visibility often reduced to the bow of the ship, collisions without some sort of foghorn were a certainty.
Before the days of radar, any distinctive noise would announce an approaching vessel or warn her away from danger areas where there were light ships, lighthouses, or warning bouys. An alarm gun might be fired at regular intervals, and gong bouys could reach the ears when one's eyes could only strain into the gray mist.

About 1850, a lengthy hand-operated cylinder had replaced earlier noise-makers. It contained a plunger with a leather washer, much like a bicycle pump. When the plunger was pulled out, then pushed in rapidly, the compressed air was vented out as long, mournful groans. This type of fog horn is still used today on ships that lack a steam whistle or the siren

TIN
HAND-OPERATED FOG
HORN USED BY CAPT
JAMES CHISAM c 1850.
ABOUT 3 FEET IN LENGTH.
(MAINE MARINE
MUSEUM, BATH)

ACTUAL SIZE.
DOG VANE OF WOODEN DISCS,
EACH WITH 8 CHICKEN FEATHERS
USED TO INDICATE DIRECTION OF
VERY LIGHT BREEZES.
(PEABODY MUSEUM OF SALEM)

foghorn.

WEATHER SIGNS AND SAYINGS ~ Of course you've heard it ~
"A red sky at night is a sailor's delight,
A red sky in the morning is the sailor's warning."
To be more specific, the veteran seagoer takes stock in these observations:

SUNRISE~ A gray sky promises a fine day, but a bright red sunrise will bring wind and possibly rain.

DAYTIME~ A light blue sky means a pleasant day, but a grayish dark-blue sky will bring heavy winds. A halo around the sun or moon means foul weather, and old salts will swear that the larger the halo, the worse it will be.

As for clouds, the more that cover the sky, the more likely that wet weather is on the way. Clouds thickening slowly tell of a siege of dismal elements. If clouds are moving east to west instead of the usual west to east, ugly weather is at hand.

Small and puffy clouds in rounded groups or lines are a mackerel sky (cirrocumulus) and bring wet weather within twenty-four

A MACKEREL SKY.

hours. The cottony billows of summer's cumulonimbus clouds bring thunderstorms and are a friend to no one. Its distance may be estimated by timing the seconds between seeing lightning and hearing its later thunder. Multiply the seconds by 0.2 to give the distance in miles. Thunderstorms travel at about twenty-five miles an hour. Thunder may be heard upward to ten miles away, and lightning may be seen at a much greater distance.

Keep a sharp eye out for sea birds flying inland, for they are seeking safety before a coming storm ~ as should all small craft.

SUNSET~ A bright yellow sunset means strong winds, while a light yellow one means rain. If copper colored, a tropical hurricane may be beyond the horizon. A diffuse and glaringly white sunset or one set behind dark clouds will bring foul weather before sunrise.

DISASTERS AT SEA

Common sea sense, proper seamanship, anticipation, and preparedness are the sailor's best defense against calamities at sea. Weather plays no favorites, and any whim of nature can freeze a sea or mine it with icebergs, or lull the crew with a calm just before a gale strikes. Three such disasters come to mind, each widely separated by time but having unanswered questions in common.

THE LOST FRANKLIN EXPEDITION, 1845~1848

One of the most haunting photographs taken in recent years turned back the pages of history to the ill-fated Franklin expedition. In 1984, researchers from the University of Alberta unearthed one of three graves from the subfreezing tundra of Canada's Beechey Island. There, staring out at the world he left nearly a century and a half earlier, was the well-preserved body of Petty Officer John Torrington. He was the first to perish in one of the worst tragedies to befall any North American exploration. Tissue samples showed that pneumonia took his life.

Gradually some answers have been discovered to this intriguing sea mystery. It began in 1845, when Sir John Franklin sailed from England to seek out the elusive Northwest Passage. It had long been known that such a route connecting the North Atlantic to the Pacific Ocean would probably be ice-locked and of no commercial value. Still, it would be a feather in anyone's tarpaulin hat if it could be proved that such a passage existed ~ if only for any scientific information that might be gleaned and for the glory of adventure in uncharted seas. The question so plagued the British Admiralty that a standing offer of ten thousand pounds was offered for such a discovery. Franklin was the man chosen to put an end to speculation, once and for all.

The fifty-eight-year-old adventurer was no stranger to polar exploration, however unsuccessful. His assistant, Captain Crozier, had also seen his share of those deep-freeze regions. Aboard their two barks (perhaps their names of "Erebus" and "Terror" were prophetic) were one hundred and twenty nine hand-picked volunteer seamen. There were supplies to last from three to five years, as well as such touches of civilization as dress uniforms, silver plate, mahogany desks, and even a grand piano. For state-of-the-art polar exploration, converted locomotive engines could supply auxiliary screws with enough power to break through the frozen ocean. And so in 1845 they sailed off to high adventure ~ never to be seen again until Torrington's photograph was taken.

THE FROZEN BODY OF JOHN TORRINGTON. NOTE HIS STRIPED SHIRT; DETAILS UNDER "CLOTHING" (FROM PHOTOGRAPH BY OWEN BEATTIE)

① WINTERED AT BEECHEY ISLAND 1845 AFTER BLOCKED BY ICE AT GRINNELL PENINSULA.
② CAUGHT IN ICE FLOES, SEPT. 1846.
③ MESSAGE LEFT ON KING WILLIAM ISLAND. FRANKLIN DIED ONE MONTH LATER.
④ ICE-LOCKED. ABANDONED SHIPS APRIL 1848.
AT ③ THEY LEAVE SECOND MESSAGE AND USELESS GEAR AND DIE TRYING TO REACH BACK RIVER.
- - - - = NORTHWEST PASSAGE AS DISCOVERED BY AMUNDSEN 1903~1905.

One of the many search parties located Franklin's first winter campsite and the three graves ~ but from there they had simply vanished. Sir John's wife needled and badgered the Admiralty to continue the search. Frustrated, she purchased a ship from her own purse and public donation and chose Captain Leopold McClintock in 1857 to seek out the truth. He was an excellent choice and had already spent seven years of his life looking for Franklin. Eighteen months later and locked in by frozen seas, he sledged over four hundred miles that included King William

Island. There, Eskimo witnesses had told of ships being crushed in the ice and their crew perishing.

McClintock stumbled on hard evidence, for the island held an amazing supply of sheet lead, heavy iron cookstoves, curtain rods, lightning conductors, and a library of religious books. Nearby were the remains of the crew who had hauled ashore, as the captain said, "... a mere accumulation of dead weight." Two notes were found, dated a year apart. The first, dated 1847, told of the two ships wintering on the ice off King William. The second, dated April 25, 1848, recorded Franklin's death that previous June and that the ships had been trapped in the ice stream for nineteen months. Nine officers and fifteen men had met their maker. The survivors were abandoning ship and were striking south ~ hopefully to the distant Hudson Bay Trading Posts.

Piece by piece, the puzzle fell into place. The expedition had sailed into that maze of barren, snow-ladened islands and then turned north. At Grinnell peninsula, a wall of ice blocked their passage. Returning southward, they managed to avoid the polar ice stream and wintered at Beechey Island. For three months, they did their best to entertain themselves (that grand piano made some sense after all) in the wintry arctic twilight and blackness. Three men died there – the first being Petty Officer Torrington.

With spring and the return of sunlight, the explorers sailed southward after the ice sheets freed their ships. A westerly passage was blocked by the polar ice stream, but a channel to the northwest of King William Island was clear enough until the ships fell in with another arm of the ice stream flowing around Victoria Island. Now prisoners of the ice stream, they were pushed no more than thirty miles in the summer of 1847. With men dying by inches and another winter ahead, they would take their chances overland to the Hudson Bay Trading Posts. The remnants were unable to drag themselves off King William Island.

Actually, Franklin's men were but sixty miles from success, for channels to the east and south of the island were free of ice and navigable. It was the Norwegian explorer Roald Amunden who took this route and sailed to the Pacific as the discoverer of the Northwest Passage in 1903.

THE KØBENHAVN VANISHES

THE KØBENHAVN.

Here was one of the finest medium clippers to ever take to the sea lanes. She was ordered built by the Danish East Asiatic Company in 1914 from Scottish shipbuilders, not long before the outbreak of World War I. Her unfinished hull was requisitioned as an oil storage hulk ~ a degrading start for a lady who should be sailing fast and free. By 1921, with her oily past behind her, a new København was launched ~ and a handsome ship she was. Affectionately known as the "Big Dane" ~ and rightly so ~ her sleek lines ran 430 feet, and she was 3965 tons. Her five steel masts rose skyward for 197 feet from the keel and were clothed in eight tons of square-rigged canvas. In case of need, her auxiliary diesel engines could move her along at six knots. Wherever she ranged, a powerful radio transmitter could keep her in touch with shores left behind.

The København had the honor of being a Danish sail-training ship. Forty-five of the crew were boy cadets from the best Danish families and averaged about seventeen years of age. The remaining hands were veteran seamen who included a sailmaker, carpenter, boatswains, and the officers. To help the school ship pay her way, the "Big Dane" carried a limited cargo. At her ports-of-call, admiring crowds turned out to see one of the few remaining tall ships (she was the last large square-rigger to be built in Britain). Many sightseers had that chance, for her nine voyages brought her to most of the ports around the world.

Her tenth voyage began as usual in Copenhagen on September 14, 1928. She had skimmed down to Buenos Aires by November 17th. Her next passage started December 14th for Gough Island for a run of 2,700 miles, and then on to Australia for a cargo of wheat.

The course would take her south to the Roaring Forties for a stern wind that should speed her along at thirteen knots (the farther south a ship sailed, the faster the trip - although this was the region of treacherous winds and icebergs and would be a calculated risk). The last contact with the København was on December 22, 1928, when she reported to passing ships that all was well and her cadets were planning a Christmas celebration when Cape Hope was sighted.

KØBENHAVN AUSTRALIA BOUND.

"ABSALON," THE "KØBENHAVN'S" FIGUREHEAD, GAVE NO PROTECTION ON THE TENTH VOYAGE.

1921

As days passed, there was only silence. The "Big Dane" had simply vanished. Concern was heightened with reports of heavy fog and icebergs in the area. Uncertainty hung over the cadets' families like a storm cloud.

Finally, many years later, a message bottle washed up on windswept Bouvet Island some 1600 miles southwest of Cape Hope. It contained a diary - probably written by a cadet. The first notation of January 20, 1929, told of five days of "terrific gales." On the 20th ~ "We have encountered icebergs all day." The following day ~ "The cold is more and more intense every hour." The entry for February 1st said that "the ice mountains seem to multiply everywhere." On the 14th of February was the distressing word that they had been drifting WESTWARD with huge icebergs in company. One week later were these terse words ~ "We have abandoned ship." The last entry on the 22nd ~ "We saw from the distance how the ship was crushed between two icebergs." His last written thoughts, while drifting helplessly in an open boat, were "Tonight in the wind and snow the captain tried to encourage us. It is snowing and a gale blows. Tonight, while everyone is sleeping, I realize our frightful fate. Everything convinces me that this sea has taken us beyond the limits of this world."

No other word or trace of the training ship was ever found.

THE "MARQUES" DISASTER

At first glance, the 117-foot "Marques" was a bark straight out of the early nineteenth century. Actually, she had once been a two-masted Spanish schooner of 1917 vintage. Converted to her new square sail rigging by the China Clipper Society of England, she saw service as a sail-training vessel. Cosmetic changes of her topside hull made her a natural for the 1976 British TV series about Charles Darwin.

But there were doubts about this maverick. According to some experts, the bark rigging had made her top-heavy with too much canvas aloft. But then, the British Department of Transportation had certified her as being seaworthy (it was learned later that no formal inspection had been done and that only the owners' surveyor had vouched for her readiness as a deep-water sailer!). And so the "Marques" was permitted to take her place in the 1984 Tall Ships Race.

Yet there were those still uneasy about her entry. Her captain was Stuart Finlay, a sailing instructor and charter-boat skipper at Antigua in the Caribbean. Although he had leased the "Marques" for the previous six months, he had not sailed other square riggers and had no captain's license. Despite nagging doubts, Finlay had every confidence in his ability to make a decent showing in the big race. He had an experienced crew of British sailors aboard in addition to the young A.S.T.A. trainees. (Race regulations state that "At least 50% of each ship's working complement must be cadets or trainees between the ages of 16 and 25, both men and women.") The skipper's wife and fifteen-month-old son were also along for the cruise.

The first leg of the Cutty Sark Inter-American Race from San Juan to Bermuda went off without a hitch. The second leg – Bermuda to Halifax – began on a flawless summer's day – the second of June. By sunset, the "Marques" had left Bermuda forty miles behind – and in rough seas. The wind was building and the barometer was dropping – a change for the worse, as any of the seasick trainees knew full well. Yet six sails were still catching wind and remained un-furled. By 4:00 A.M. heavy rain drenched the rolling deck, then abruptly ceased after five minutes. The wind no longer whistled in the rigging, the sails went limp, and stars replaced the rolling black clouds.

Then, like a wrathful sea monster, a violent squall hit the "Marques" port broadside. The seas, driven into mountainous waves, swept the deck and flooded into the open hatches. In her death throes, the bark heeled far over on her starboard. The bow dove into a wall of water and then was gone. Those on deck had a fighting chance to free themselves from the tangle of rigging as the vessel took her final plunge. Those below deck had almost no chance to escape from their quarters.

At 5:00 A.M., a Polish yawl spotted flares from the survivors' life raft (these self-inflating rubber rafts are standard equipment on any windjammer). High winds prevented her from coming about, but her "mayday" message did bring the Polish schooner "Zawisza Czarny" to the rescue. In the scattering of the "Marques" wreckage were nine survivors safe on the rafts and an overturned dinghy. Nineteen had perished, the victims of poor seamanship and not anticipating the changing weather.

DISASTER IN THE GALLEY

Salt air and heavy deck work can build up a powerful appetite. But on the old square-riggers, the cook, like a sea witch over her caldron, could only brew up a monotonous and frequently undigestable fare. The day's "menu" would likely include "salt horse" or "salt junk." Before the days of refrigeration, dried beef and pork layered with salt and saltpeter would be loaded aboard in three-hundred-pound casks. It was as red as a sailor's flannel shirt. It was so hard and tough that the crew sometimes carved snuff boxes and trinkets from the salt beef. When polished, they looked very much like mahogany.

To make the chunks pliable, they were placed in a "harness cask" and soaked in sea water for a day or so. Before soaking, the meat did indeed resemble a horse's harness. Once boiled, sooner or later at a meal, some old Jack Tar would impale a piece with his sheath knife. Reverently raising it above his head, he would recite these lines—

A "HARNESS CASK" WITH A WIDE BASE TO PREVENT CAPSIZING. BRASS HARDWARE.

"Old horse! Old horse! what brought you here?
From Sacarap' to Portland pier
I carted stone for many a year.
I labored long and well, alack,
'Till I fell down and broke my back.
They picked me up with sore abuse
And salted me down for sailor's use.
The sailors they do me despise,
They pick me up and damn my eyes,
They eat my flesh and gnaw my bones
And throw the rest to Davy Jones."

It was said that cooked salt beef was as dry as a captain's Sunday sermon and could skin the roof of one's mouth until it had become calloused like a sailor's hands. Sometimes it was thinly disguised in a reasonably savory dish called "lobscouse." Hard tack was powdered with an iron fid. Dried peas— hard and black as musket balls—were added along with any other vegetables, as potatoes, that happened by. Salt meat was cut into small pieces and tossed in. Boiled and seasoned, it was a diner's delight.

~RECIPE FOR HARD TACK~
MIX 1 TEASPOON SALT WITH 1 POUND FLOUR, AND ENOUGH WATER TO MAKE A VERY STIFF DOUGH. DIVIDE INTO 4-INCH SECTIONS AND PUNCH WITH HOLES. BAKE IN A FLAT PAN AT 250° FOR 2-3 HOURS.

HARD TACK WAS ALSO ROUND-SHAPED.

Hard tack (white bread was soft tack and a rarity on a nineteenth-century ship) seemed fit company for "salt junk," for both were flint hard and jaw breakers. The English called them "dog biscuits" and, if jam was available, would make "cracker hash." After pounding to a pulp and extracting any weevils, water and jam were added. After stirring well, the mixture was baked in a pan— if the cook was in good spirits and agreeable.

"Duff" was widely appreciated, and rumbles of mutiny could be avoided by serving it at least once a week. Flour, lard, and yeast— and sometimes finely chopped pork— were boiled in equal parts of fresh and salt water until the mixture was firm. Molasses topped the finished delicacy.

Molasses was used for all sweetening because it was cheaper than sugar. It was added to the hot coffee, tea, or chocolate that was usually available after the watch or at mealtime. The American merchantmen, according to Dana, favored the proportions of one pint of tea and a pint and a half of molasses to three gallons of water before boiling. As for rum rations, the temperance movement in the nineteenth century gradually phased out this sort of liquid refreshment. "Temperance ships," as most were, found the crews satisfied and less troublesome when a plentiful supply of hot coffee or tea was at hand.

Freshly caught fish made a welcome change in the diet, and fresh fruits and vegetables were stocked when in port. Potatoes were valued, for they resisted spoilage and were one of the few sources of scurvy-preventing vitamin C on a long voyage. Today, refrigeration has made the old sea fare a memory that is less than inspiring. The "Eagle," for example, carries a thirty-day supermarket of fresh and frozen food and has an additional six-month supply of canned food stores.

SPARE TIME

SCRIMSHAW IS AN OLD NEW ENGLAND TERM FOR KILLING TIME. NOW IT STANDS FOR MAKING OR DECORATING BONE OR IVORY ARTICLES.

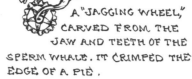

A "JAGGING WHEEL," CARVED FROM THE JAW AND TEETH OF THE SPERM WHALE. IT CRIMPED THE EDGE OF A PIE.

IT TOOK SEVERAL VOYAGES BEFORE A SHIP MODEL COULD BE FINISHED. USUALLY ONE TO THREE FEET LONG, THEY WERE FINELY RIGGED BUT OFTEN OUT OF SCALE.

NANTUCKET ISLAND BEGAN USING AN OVAL OR ROUND WOODEN BASKET BOTTOM IN 1840. RATTAN (CANE OR REED), BROUGHT BY WHALERS FROM THE FAR EAST, WAS USED FOR WEAVING. NANTUCKET'S SOUTH SHOAL LIGHTSHIP MADE MANY OF THESE.

FANCY WOVEN MAT OF DYED ROPE YARN.

A SCRUB-DOWN WITH COLD SEA WATER.

IT WAS BAD LUCK TO KILL AN ALBATROSS.

THE ALBATROSS WAS A GREAT SEA BIRD WITH WINGSPREADS OF UP TO FIFTEEN FEET AND A HEAD LARGE ENOUGH TO WEAR AN APPRENTICE'S HAT. THEY WERE CAUGHT WITH A "V"-SHAPED PIECE OF TIN ON A LINE AND BAITED WITH SALT PORK. WHEN ITS HOOKED BILL CAUGHT IN THE "V," IT TOOK THREE MEN TO HAUL IT ABOARD. SINCE THEY NEEDED A RUNNING START TO FLY, THEY REMAINED ON DECK AS PETS.

THE SHARK'S TAIL WAS NAILED TO THE BOWSPRIT AS A WARNING TO ITS KIND. CHUNKS WERE CUT AND THROWN TO ITS FELLOWS.

THE HATED SHARK WAS A MENACE TO ALL SAILORS, AND ITS DECKING WAS AN EVENT. HIS GLARING EYES AND VICIOUS TEETH HELD NO FEAR ONCE A BUTCHER'S CLEAVER HAD SEVERED THE SPINE FROM THE HEAD. THE VERTEBRAE WERE DRIED AND THREADED ON A THIN METAL ROD FOR A WALKING STICK. THE TEETH WOULD BECOME SOUVENIRS AND THE SKIN MADE INTO POUCHES. THE LIVER'S OIL PREVENTED WET STIFF HANDS FROM CRACKING.

FAMILIAR SEA TALK ~ as heard aboard.

VIKING STEER BOARD.

"Port" ~ The left side of the ship - the loading side in port.

"Starboard" ~ The right side of the ship. The Vikings used a steer board or right-sided rudder.

"Furl" ~ to be made in a bundle (old English "furdle").

"Taken aback" ~ to be surprised or astounded. When tacking into the wind, the sails may be suddenly and violently blown back against the mast.

"Crow's-nest" ~ a protected lookout near the top of the mainmast. In ancient days, crows were caged there and released when visibility was poor and the ship's location in doubt. The crow flew straight for land and the ship followed.

"Running afoul" ~ to be entangled in conflict or collision as when the rigging and spars became entangled.

"Shrouds" ~ rope supports for the masts. When rope was of poor quality on early ships, so many were needed that they looked like a shroud covering the dead.

"Mind your P's and Q's" ~ keep your affairs in order and don't run up debts. Some taverns extended credit to sailors. A chalkboard with headings of "P" for pints and "Q" for quarts was checked off next to the seaman's name. The tally was kept 'til payday.

"Above board" ~ honest and nothing to hide. The ship's "board" was her side and entirely visible.

"Between wind and water" ~ a vulnerable position, as when the ship rolled and exposed the hull below the waterline.

"To be all at sea" ~ to be confused.

"Salt junk" ~ was salt meat. The fibers of a rope were called junk, much like the stringy, tough salt beef or pork.

"Bitter end" ~ a disastrous and final finish. The bitter end of a rope was its short end when secured to a bitt (deck post.)

"Flattering weather" ~ not to be trusted, as the calm before a squall.

"Cut of his jib" ~ to size up another's features. Jibsails at the bow often told of a ship's nationality. Spain might have a small jib or none at all, the English but one, and the French often two. This often referred to another's nose, for like the jibsail, it was the first to arrive.

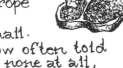

"Show a leg" ~ shed the covers and get going. In past centuries when some "wives" went along on a long voyage, the watch boatswain called for a show of legs from the bunks. Owners of a shapely feminine limb need not "rise (it used to be rouse) and shine." "Turn to" had a like meaning and "turn in" was the welcome bedtime call.

"Shoot Charlie Noble" ~ this was the name for the galley smoke-pipe and was cleaned by firing a pistol up into the pipe.

"Bowsprit" ~ to "sprout" (old Saxon) as sprouting from the bow.

"Wet your whistle" ~ a drink of the harder stuff.

"Three sheets to the wind" ~ dead drunk. (A sheet was the rope or chain attached to the lower corners of the sail.).

"Spinning a yarn" ~ telling tall stories. When deck work lagged, the crew was put to work separating the fibers or "yarns" from old rope for caulking. It was a chance to swap stories.

"Not room to swing a cat" ~ low headroom and not cruelty to animals. The boatswain needed enough space to swing his cat-o-nine-tails whip for punishment.

"Ditty bag" ~ a small canvas bag for stowing small gear. Possibly from the Saxon "dite" meaning tidy.

An anchor to the windward" ~ a thrifty sailor.

"Slipped his cable" ~ he died. (The cable moored or anchored a ship.)

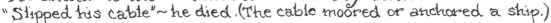

THE TALL SHIP RACES

It was June, 1976 ~ America's first real viewing of the Tall Ship fleet. 350,000 enthusiastic American Bicentennial spectators choked the streets and shorefront of Newport, Rhode Island. It seemed the island would sink under the crowds. OpSail '76 had begun with a gathering of the tall ships at Plymouth, England. On the way to America, there was a stopover at Teneriffe, largest of the Canary Islands, for a brief interchange of crews. Since 1964, this shipmate swap had been a feature of the Tall Ship races, and a boy or girl could sample a different size ship, foreign speech, and different customs. Each was an ambassador of international good will and understanding. It was reported that when the USCG "Eagle" took part in the exchange, there were eleven different languages being spoken aboard!

MIRCEA

CHRISTIAN RADICH

GAZELA PRIMEIRO

SAGRES

After a short sail to another island port, the crews returned to their own ships. The race was on, and competition keen on the transatlantic run. Bermuda was the port of call before racing off to Newport. But there were problems at the mile-long Bermuda starting line. The eighteen large windjammers had bunched themselves at the favorable windward end and well away from a dangerous reef. The oldest vessel in the fleet, the "Gazela Primeiro," found herself between the "Mircea" and the "Christian Radich." The "Mircea" held her course and sheared off the "Gazela Primeiro's" main-topmast with her bowsprit. Although forced into the "Christian Radich," neither ship suffered from the brushing.

Farther ahead, the "Libertad" and the "Juan Sebastian" had run afoul. The "Libertad's" mainsail had been split and her port lifeboats swept overboard. The "Juan Sebastian" had the worst of it, for her fore-stay had become caught in the other's yardarm. Backing off, her topmast was severed. More than that, a

JUAN SEBASTIAN DE ELCANO

LIBERTAD

cadet aloft fell and was injured. Fortunately, he landed on the collapsing canvas and not the deck.

Captain Jurkiewicz of Poland's "Dar Pomorza" remarked at the time that "I avoided accident because I have learned not to take unnecessary risks. A whole fleet of students watched those collisions today. I hope they all gained a lesson in seamanship."

But ahead lay Narragansett Bay and Newport Harbor with all her well-wishers. The recreated eighteenth-century "H.M.S. Rose" was also there to welcome the newer-vintage tall ships. She was a reminder of Revolutionary War days when the British—and then the French—fleets anchored in the bay. Two hundred years later, Newport's skies were again crowded with sail, and the town celebrated the event with parades, fireworks, and ship visiting. Then the fleet sailed off to New York City for another round of red, white, and blue merrymaking. OPSail '76, a separate entity from the A.S.T.A. and S.T.A., ran the shore-related activities. All in all, it was quite a birthday party!

The Tall Ship Races didn't just happen. Bernard Morgan, a London solicitor, was distressed by the decline of the cargo-carrying windjammers in the 1950s. Those splendid square-riggers had more than proven their worth as sail-training ships. If those sea-going schools were to have a friendly race, perhaps the public

1976 "BICENTENNIAL ERA THE SEAFARING TRADITION" ENVELOPE.
REDUCED FROM 4x9½ INCHES. THE POSTAGE WAS SMALLER AS WELL!

would again value them for character-building potential. After considerable button-holing, the idea caught fire. By 1956, twenty-one ships from eleven countries crossed the starting line at Torbay, England, for what was thought to be a one-time race. By the time the finish line at Lisbon, Portugal, was in sight, there were believers everywhere. An unqualified success, the newly formed Sail Training Association began planning competitive sailings as a yearly event.

Race destinations in the following years gave a hint of the adventures that awaited new sail trainees ~ Southsea ~ Cherbourg ~ Copenhagen ~ Gothenburg ~ Den Helder ~ Kristiansand ~ Canary Islands and St. Malo. In 1972, Barclay Warburton thought America should have a hand in the excitement. He sailed his small brigantine (as said before and worth repeating) across the Atlantic to join that year's race. His enthusiasm was contagious, and within three years the American Sail Training Association was in business. As an affiliate of the S.T.A., the A.S.T.A. would manage the Tall Ship Races on this side of the Atlantic ~ and just in time for our Bicentennial.

There followed such Tall Ship Races as that from Boston to Kristiansand. It was Boston's 350th anniversary, and the influx of tall ship spectators was so great (upward to five million!) that a state of emergency was declared. OP Sail '86 will see a tall ship visit to New York City ~ July 3rd to the 8th ~ for a gigantic birthday party for the century-old Statue of Liberty. The tall ships will be a part of Australia's Bicentennial in 1987~88. Not to be missed will be the Tall Ship Race in 1992 ~ the 500th anniversary of Columbus' voyage to America. Spain, Italy, and North and South America will share that historic year.

Race participants are divided into three classes. CLASS A includes all square-riggers longer than 120 feet and other sailers longer than 160 feet. Generally these are navy or merchant navy ships. CLASS A, Division II has all square-rigged vessels less than 120 feet in length. CLASS B has all fore-and-aft-rigged vessels between 100 and 160 feet in length. This class usually is made up of sailing-school, oceanographic research and commercial sailers. CLASS C accepts all other sailing craft with a waterline length of over 30 feet. These are mostly private yachts that take young people aboard just for the races.

And speaking of young people, at least fifty percent of each vessel's working complement must be cadets or trainees between the ages of sixteen and twenty-five, both men and women.

THE TALL SHIP MARK OF THE A.S.T.A.

The International Sail Training Races for all classes are held in even years. The A.S.T.A. also races B and C in odd years.

TALL SHIP IDENTIFICATION~ Class A Sail Trainers

SHIP

"DAR MŁODZIEŻY" POLAND, NAVY~ 357'6"~
CREW 166-196 ~ BUILT 1982 DURING POLAND'S
SOLIDARITY MOVEMENT. REPLACED DAR POMORZA.
* PROMINENT DECK HOUSES. BLACK HULL LINE.
DOES NOT HAVE MEDIUM CLIPPER LINES.

SHIP

AMERIGO VESPUCCI ~ ITALY, NAVY ~
333' ~ CREW 500 ~ BUILT 1931 ITALY ~
* STEEL BUT LOOKS LIKE 19TH CENTURY
FRIGATE. HULL HAS 2 WIDE WHITE STRIPES.

SHIP

"LIBERTAD"~ARGENTINA, NAVY~298'~
CREW 366~ BUILT 1963 ARGENTINA.
* LARGE MAIN DECK HOUSE, HIGH FOR-
WARD PILOTHOUSE, LOW RIG.
GREEN SAILS.

SHIP

"SØRLANDET"~ NORWAY MERCHANT~
216'~ CREW 95 CADETS*~
BUILT 1927 NORWAY, * FINE LINES.

SHIP

"DANMARK"~ DENMARK MERCHANT~
213'~ BUILT 1932 DENMARK~
* SIMILAR TO CHRISTIAN RADICH. FINE!

SHIP

"CHRISTIAN RADICH"~ NORWAY
MERCHANT~206'~ CREW 104'~
BUILT 1937 NORWAY, FINE.

SHIP

"GEORG STAGE"~ DENMARK
MERCHANT~135'~CREW 80
TRAINEES'~ BUILT 1934
DENMARK. FINE LINES.

BARK

"SEDOV"~ RUSSIA, NAVY~358'~ CREW ?~
BUILT 1921 GERMANY * IT IS FEARED THAT
HER FINE LINES MAY NOW BE ALTERED.

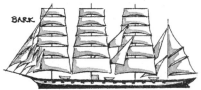

BARK

"KRUZENSHTERN"~ RUSSIA MERCHANT~ 342'~
CREW 236~ BUILT 1926 GERMANY * BLACK
HULL WITH WHITE STRIPE THAT HIGHLIGHTS
"GUN" PORTS. SISTER SHIP OF "PEKING"
AT NEW YORK CITY.

BARK

"STATSRAAD LEHMKUHL"~ NORWAY MERCHANT~
287'~ CREW 204~ BUILT 1914 GERMANY~

BARK

"NIPPON MARU"~ JAPAN, MERCHANT~ 365'~
CREW 168~ BUILT 1930 JAPAN * UNUSUALLY
HIGH FREEBOARD GIVE MORE SUNLIGHT TO
CADET CLASSROOMS.

BARK

"SEA CLOUD"~ CAYMAN ISLANDS, COMMERCIAL
PASSENGER~ 316'~ CREW 60 ~ GUESTS 75~
BUILT 1931 GERMANY~ * HEAVY DECK HOUSE
ADDITIONS HAVE CHANGED HER FINE LINES.

BARK

"CUAUHTEMOC"~ MEXICO, NAVY ~ 268'~ CREW 185 ~ BUILT 1982 SPAIN ~ * WELL DECK AND NO DECK HOUSE.

BARK

"SIMON BOLIVAR"~ VENEZUELA, NAVY ~ 270'~ CREW 194 ~ BUILT 1980 SPAIN * BLACK "GUN" PORTS BETWEEN BLACK HULL LINES.

BARK

"MIRCEA"~ ROMANIA, NAVY ~ 269'5'~ CREW 107~ BUILT 1938 GERMANY.

BARK

"SAGRES"~ PORTUGAL, NAVY ~ 268'~ CREW 203'~ BUILT 1937 GERMANY. * PORTUGUESE CROSS OF CHRIST ON SAILS.

BARK

"GUAYAS"~ ECUADOR, NAVY~ 268'~ CREW 115 ~ BUILT 1977 SPAIN~ *LARGE FLYING BRIDGE AFT. HULL SIMILAR TO "SIMON BOLIVAR."

BARK

"EAGLE"~ USA, COAST GUARD ~ 266'~ CREW 189 ~ BUILT 1936 GERMANY * DISTINCTIVE BOW RED SLANTED BAND WITH EMBLEM. AND THINNER BLUE STRIPE. SISTER SHIP IS THE "SAGRES." NEAR SISTERS ARE THE "MIRCEA," "GORCH FOCK," AND THE "TOVARITSCH."

BARK

"GORCH FOCK," ~ GERMANY, NAVY~ 266'~ CREW 173'~ BUILT 1958 GERMANY * GOLD-BROWN 6'WIDE STRIPE ON HULL GIVES A PLEASING APPEARANCE.

BARK

"TOVARISHCH"~ RUSSIA, NAVY~ 240'~ CREW 190 ~ BUILT 1933 GERMANY.

BARK

"GLORIA"~ COLUMBIA, NAVY ~ 225'~ CREW 115 ~ BUILT 1968 SPAIN ~ * GREEN TRIM, GREEN AND GOLD STERN-BOARD, AFTER CABIN HAS GOLD WORK AND A MUSEUM OF COUNTRY'S ARTIFACTS.

TOPSAIL SCHOONER

"ESMERALDA"~ CHILE, NAVY~ 308.5'~ CREW 332 ~ BUILT 1952 SPAIN. SISTER SHIP TO SPAIN'S "JUAN SEBASTIAN DE ELCANO. * CONDOR FIGUREHEAD WON'T BE FORGOTTEN!

TOPSAIL SCHOONER

"JUAN SEBASTIAN DE ELCANO"~ SPAIN, NAVY ~ 304'~ CREW 407~ BUILT 1927 SPAIN~ * HULL SIMILAR TO "ESMERALDA."

BARK

"ELISSA~ USA, GALVESTON SAIL TRAINER~ 160.5'~ CREW ?~ BUILT 1877.

BARKENTINE

"GAZELA PRIMEIRO"~ USA PHILA. MARITIME MUSEUM~155'5'~ CREW?~ BUILT 1886 PORTUGAL *WOOD HULL.

SOURCES OF INFORMATION ON SAIL TRAINING

Association of Sea Training Organizations
40 Royal Yachting Association
Victoria Way, Woking
Surrey GU21 1EQ, England

The American Sail Training Association
P.O. Box 1459
47 Bowen's Wharf
Newport, Rhode Island 02840

California Maritime Academy
P.O. Box 1392
Vallejo, California 93490

Great Lakes Maritime Academy
Northwest Michigan College
Traverse City, Michigan 49684

Maine Maritime Academy
Castine, Maine 04421

Massachusetts Maritime Academy
Buzzards Bay, Massachusetts 02532

Texas Maritime Academy
Galveston, Texas 77553

U.S. Merchant Marine Academy
Kings Point, New York 11024

*See ASTA's booklet "Sail Training Ships
and Programs Directory" for complete
programs and addresses.*

SELECTED NORTH AMERICAN MARITIME MUSEUMS

California

Los Angeles Maritime Museum, Berth 84, foot of 6th St., San Pedro, CA 90731. Maritime history and archaeology, ship building, maritime cultures, naval trade, and fishing history displayed in an old ferry building: Tues.–Sat., 10–5; closed Thanksgiving and Christmas. No charge.

Maritime Museum of Monterey, 5 Custom House Plaza, Monterey, CA 93940. Maritime artifacts, ship models, paintings, and photographs. Daily, 10–5; closed New Year's Day, Thanksgiving, and Christmas. Admission charge.

San Diego Maritime Museum, 1306 N. Harbor Dr., Sand Diego, CA 92101. Collections of ship models, navigational instruments and tools, U.S. navy artifacts, marine engineering, and small crafts. Three historic ships: 1863 *Star of India*, 1898 ferryboat *Berkeley*, and 1904 steam yacht *Medea*. Daily, 9–8. Admission charge.

San Francisco Maritime National Historical Park, Hyde Street Pier, San Francisco, CA 94109. Photographs, plans, log books, ship models, and ship artifacts, historic ships: square-rigged ship *Balclutha*, schooner *C.A. Thayer*, ferry *Eureka*, steamer tug *Hercules*, scow schooner *Alma*, and paddle-wheel tug *Eppleton Hall*, all at Hyde Street Pier. The clipper-bowed fishing boat *Monterey* and the steam schooner *Wapama* are at the Sausalito water front. Museum building, daily, 10–5; Hyde Street Pier mid-September–mid-May, 9:30–5; mid-May–mid-September, 10–6. Admission charge.

Treasure Island Museum, 410 Palm Avenue, Treasure Island, San Francisco, CA 94130-0413. The 1939 Golden Gate International Exposition building contains artifacts relating to the sea services in the Pacific. Daily, 10–10:30. Closed New Year's Day, Thanksgiving, and Christmas. No charge.

Ventura County Maritime Museum, Inc., 2731 South Victoria Avenue, Oxnard, CA 93035. Ship models, 17th-to-20th-century maritime art, shipboard gear, prototype boats, and local maritime history. Thursday–Monday, 11–5. Closed New Year's, Thanksgiving, and Christmas. No charge.

Connecticut

Connecticut River Museum, 67 Main Street, Essex, CT 06426. Small craft, marine archaeology, working model of the first submarine, the American Turtle, and the 1813 chandlery. Tues.–Sun., 10–5. Admission charge.

The Maritime Center at Norwalk, 10 N. Water Street, Norwalk, CT 06854. Aquarium of marine life indigenous to Long Island Sound, boat-building tools, oystering, and navigation. Sept.–May, 10–5; June–Aug., daily, 10–6. Closed New Year's Day and Christmas Day. Admission charge.

Mystic Seaport, 75 Greenmanville Ave., Mystic, CT 06355-0990. At this 19th-century shipyard site are historic buildings in a New England maritime village setting, six historic ships, children's museum, shipyard and boat-building shop, small craft displays, and a vast 19th-century collection of marine artifacts, art, plans, maps, and charts. April–June, daily, 9–5; July–Aug.,

9–8; Sept.–Dec, 9–5; Jan.–Mar., 9–4. Closed Christmas. Admission charge.

U.S. Coast Guard Museum, U.S. Coast Guard Academy, 15 Mohegan Ave., New London, CT 06320-4195. The maritime museum details the U.S. Coast Guard and its predecessors, the revenue Cutter Service, Lighthouse Service, and the Life-Saving Service. Mon.–Fri., 9–4:30; Sat., 10–5; Sun, 12–5. Closed national holidays. No charge.

Delaware

Treasures of the Sea Exhibit, Rte. 18, Delaware Technical & Community College, Georgetown, DE 19947. Museum exhibits shipwreck artifacts, coin firearms, jewelry, gold and silver bars, and cannons. Mon.–Tues., 10–4; Friday, 12–4; Sat., 9–1. Closed national holidays and Christmas break. Admission charge.

District of Columbia

The Navy Museum, 901 M St. S.E., Washington, D.C. 20374-5060. Displayed in an old naval gun factory are weapons, artifacts, scientific instruments, maps, prints, flags, uniforms, nautical memorabilia. Mon.–Fri., 9–4; Sat.–Sun. and holidays, 10–4. Closed New Year's, Thanksgiving, Christmas Eve and Day. No charge.

Florida

Mel Fisher Maritime Heritage Society, 200 Green St., Key West, FL 33040. 17th–18th century coins, ceramics, slave-trade and maritime artifacts. Daily, 9:30–5. Admission charge.

Ponce De Leon Inlet Lighthouse Preservation Association, Inc. 4931 S. Peninsula Drive, Ponce Inlet, FL 32127. Exhibits displayed in an 1890 lighthouse, three keepers' houses, and four out-buildings. Daily, 10–5. Admission charge.

St. Augustine Lighthouse Museum, 81 Lighthouse Ave., St. Augustine, FL 32085. Maritime and historical museum. Daily, 9–5. Closed Thanksgiving and Christmas. Admission charge.

Georgia

Confederate Naval Museum, 202 4th St., Columbus, GA 31902. Exhibits include the Confederate naval gunboats CSS *Jackson* and CSS *Chattahoochee*. Tues.–Fri., 10–5; Sat.–Sun., 1–5. Closed major holidays. No charge.

Ships of the Sea Maritime Museum, 503 East River Street, Savannah, GA 31401. In restored waterfront cotton warehouse are displayed ship models, figureheads, scrimshaw, historical artifacts, and ships chandlery. Daily, 10–5. Admission charge.

U.S. Navy Supply Corps Museum, U.S. Navy Supply Corps School, 1425 Prince Ave., Athens, GA 30606-2205. U.S. naval history, uniforms, navigational equipment, gallery gear, ship models, personal memorabilia. Mon.–Fri., 9–5. Closed federal holidays. No charge.

Maine

Kittery Historical and Naval Museum, Rogers Road, Kittery, ME 03904. Ship models, shipbuilding, regional archaeology. June–Oct., Mon.–Fri., 10–4. Admission charge.

Maine Maritime Museum, 243 Washington St., Bath, ME 04530. Maine maritime history in historic, 19th-century shipyard showing tools, equipment, shipping, small craft center, river cruises. Daily, 9:30–5. Closed New Year's Day, Thanksgiving, and Christmas. Admission charge.

Penobscot Marine Museum, Church St., Searsport, ME 04974-0498. The old town hall and three former shipmasters' homes display ship models, a small craft collection, shipbuilding tools, navigational instruments, and whaling memorabilia. Memorial Day–mid-Oct., Mon.–Sat., 9:30–5; Sun., 1–5. Admission charge.

Sailor's Memorial Museum, Grindle Point, Islesboro, ME 04848. An 1850 lighthouse and keepers house exhibit marine artifacts and history. Mid-June–Labor Day, Tues.–Sun., 10–4. No charge.

Shore Village Museum, 104 Limerock St., Rockland, ME 04841. The lighthouse museum contains lighthouse and marine artifacts, nautical instruments, Coast Guard gear, scrimshaw, lobstering tools and ship models. June–mid-Oct., daily, 10–4. No charge.

Maryland

Baltimore Maritime Museum, Pier III, Pratt St., Baltimore, MD 21202. Lighthouse Service, U.S. Navy, and the U.S. Coast Guard museum displays. Also three historic steam vessels. Mon.–Thurs. 9:30–5; Fri.–Sun., 9:30–7. Closed New Year's Day, Thanksgiving, and Christmas. Admission charge.

Calvert Marine Museum, 14200 Solomons Island Rd., Solomons, MD 20688. Marine history and artifacts, small craft, historic 1899 boat, and log-built oyster boat. Daily, 10–5. Closed New Year's Day, Thanksgiving, and Christmas. Admission charge.

Chesapeake Bay Maritime Museum, Navy Point, St. Michaels, MD 21663. Historic ships, artifacts and decoys of the Chesapeake Bay area, aquarium, lighthouse, and boatyard. May–Oct., daily, 10–5; Nov.–Dec., daily, 10–4; Jan.–Mar., Sat.–Sun., 10–4. Closed New Year's Day, Thanksgiving, and Christmas. Admission charge.

St. Clements Island—Potomac River Museum, Breezepoint Rd., Point, MD 20626. Maritime collections, Indian and local history. Late Mar.–Memorial Day, Mon.–Fri., 9–5, Sat.–Sun., 10–5; Oct.–late March, Wed.–Sun., 12–4. Closed New Year's Day, Thanksgiving, and Christmas Day. Admission charge.

Massachusetts

Beverly Historical Society and Museum, 117 Cabot St., Beverly, MA 01915. Maritime, military, and general. Wed.–Sat., 10–4. Closed holidays. Admission charge.

Cape Ann Historical Society and Museum, 27 Pleasant St., Gloucester, MA 01930. 19th-century maritime history, art, fisheries artifacts, historic vessels. March–Jan., Tues.–Sat., 10-5. Closed holidays. Admission charge.

The Custom House Maritime Museum of Newburyport, 25 Water St., Newburyport, MA 01950. Maritime artifacts, 19th-century objects from foreign trade, navigational tools, instruments, and maritime history of the Merrimac Valley. April–Dec., Mon.–Sat., 10–4; Sun., 1–4. Admission charge.

Essex Shipbuilding Museum, 28 Main St., Essex, MA 01929. Shipbuilding half-molds, 1927 fishing schooner, sailing memorabilia. May–Oct., Thurs.–Mon., 10–4. Admission charge.

Kendall Whaling Museum, 27 Everett St., Sharon, MA 02067. Whaling equipment, scrimshaw, logbooks, figureheads, and foreign trade relics. Tues.–Sat. and Mon. holidays, 10-5. Closed New Year's, Memorial Day, Independence Day, Thanksgiving, and Christmas. Admission charge.

Maritime Museum, 4 Elm St., Cohasset, MA 02025. Shipwreck and life-saving equipment, 19th-century maritime artifacts, sailing-ship models, shipbuilding, Minot's Ledge lighthouse. June–late Sept., Tues.–Sun., 1:30–4:30. No charge.

The MIT Museum, 265 Massachusetts Ave., Cambridge, MA 02139. Hart Nautical Gallery science and technology, rigged and half models, prints, and photographs. Sept.–June, Tues. and Thurs.–Fri., 12–6; Wed., 12–8; Sat.–Sun., 1-5. Closed holidays. No charge.

Salem Maritime National Historic Site, 174 Derby St., Salem, MA 01970. 1765 Derby Wharf, 1790 Central Wharf, 1819 Custom house, 1819 bonded warehouse, 1829 scale house, circa 1800 West India goods store, 1761 Derby house, circa 1670 Narbonne-Hale house, 1775 and 1801 Derby-Hawks house. Daily and holidays, 9–5. Closed New Year's Day, Thanksgiving, and Christmas. No charge.

USS *Constitution*, Charlestown, MA 02129. Old Ironsides, launched 1797, world's oldest commissioned warship, rigging, cannon, and ship's gear. Daily, 9:30–3:50. Guided tours, unguided top-deck tours, 3:50–sunset. Morning and evening colors ceremony, 8 A.M. and sunset. No charge.

Michigan

Dossin Great Lakes Museum, 100 Strand Dr., Belle Isle, Detroit, MI 48207. Ship models, artifacts, restored steamer interior, and freighter pilot house, Wed.–Sun., 10–4. Closed national holidays. No charge.

Le Sault de Sainte Marie Historical Sites, Inc., 501 E. Water St., Sault Ste. Marie, MI 49783. Great Lakes maritime items. Mid-May–June and Sept.–mid-Oct., daily, 10–6; July–Aug, daily, 9–9. Admission charge.

Michigan Maritime Museum, Dyckman at Bridge South Haven, MI 49090. Historic vessels, models, marine art and tools, and historic life-saving station. May–Sept., Tues.–Sun., 10–5; Oct.–April, Wed.–Sat., 10–4. Admission charge.

Minnesota

Split Rock Historic Site and History Center, 2010 Hwy. 61

East. Two Harbors, MN 55616. Exhibits on lighthouses and marine navigation at 1900 light station. Mid-May–mid-Oct, daily, 9–5; mid-Oct.–mid-May, Fri.–Sun., 12–4. Closed Easter and Christmas. Admission charge.

Mississippi

Maritime and Seafood Industry Museum, 115 First St., Bilox, MS 39530. Objects and instruments used in the seafood industry, two sixty-five-foot replicated Biloxi schooners, boatbuildnig, hurricane-exhibit room. Mon.–Sat., 9–5. Closed New Year's Day, Mardi Gras, Memorial Day, Independence Day, Thanksgiving, and Christmas. Admission charge.

New Jersey

Historic Gardner's Basin, 800 N. New Hampshire Ave., and the Bay, Atlantic City, NJ 08401. Maritime artifacts, seafaring memorabilia, lobstering. Closed New Year's Day and Christmas. No charge.

New York

The Antique Boat Museum, 750 Mary St., Clayton, NY 13624. Historic boats of the Thousand Islands region. Mid-May–mid-Oct., daily, 9–4. Admission charge.

East Hampton Town Marine Museum, 101 Main St., East Hampton, NY 11937. Whaling and fishing museum, small craft, and archaeology of eastern Long Island. Memorial Day–Labor Day, daily, 10–5. Admission charge.

Historical Society of Greater Port Washington, 115 Prospect St., Port Jefferson, NY 11777. Half hulls, sailmaker's tools and loft, shipbuilding tools, paintings, local marine history. Memorial Day–Labor Day, Sat.–Sun, 1–4; July–Aug., Sat.–Sun.; and Tues.–Wed., 1–4. Admission charge.

Long Island Maritime Museum, 86 West Ave., West Sayville, NY 11796. Maritime history; small craft collection, life equipment, shipwreck artifacts, historical buildings and three ships. Wed.–Sat., 10–3; Sun., 12–4. Closed Monday during winter months and national holidays. Admission charge.

Sackets Harbor Battlefield State Historic Site, 505 W. Washington St., Sackets Harbor, NY 13685. Historic U.S. Navy Yard and battlefield site with collections housed in six early 19th-century buildings, weapons, naval artifacts, maritime museum, and restored Navy yard complex. Mid-May–mid-September, Tues.–Sat., 10–5; Sun., 1–5. No charge.

Sag Harbor Whaling and Historical Museum, Main St., Sag Harbor, NY 11963. Housed in an 1845 house are whaling tools, scrimshaw, fishing gear, and general antiques. Children's museum and whaleboat. Mid-May–Sept., Mon.–Sat., 10–5; Sun. 1–5. Admission charge.

Sodus Bay Historical Society, 7606 N. Ontario St., Sodus Point, NY 14555. Lighthouse museum with collections on Lake Ontario and Sodus Bay. May–Oct., Tues.–Sun., 10–5. Open Monday holidays. No charge.

The South Street Seaport Museum, 207 Front St., New York, NY 10038. Historic four-masted bark, square-rigged ship, wooden fishing schooner, light ship, schooner, and a steam ferryboat. Museum collections in archaeology, ship models, nautical artifacts, navigational instruments, fish-market displays. July–Labor Day, daily, 10–6; Labor Day–June, daily, 10–5. Admission charge.

Whaling Museum Society Inc., Cold Spring Harbor Whaling Museum, Main St., Box 25, Cold Spring Harbor, NY 11724. Scrimshaw, ship model, maritime paintings, 19th-century whaleboat, whaling gear, Long Island whaling, and marine-mammal-conservation display. Memorial Day–Labor Day, daily, 11–5; Labor Day–Memorial Day, Tue.–Sun., 11–5. Admission charge.

Ohio

Fairport Marine Museum, 129 Second St., Fairport Harbor, OH 44077. Collections in the 1871 lighthouses include navigational instruments, charts, shipbuilding tools, and models. Memorial Day–Oct., Wed.–Sun., and legal holidays, 1–6. Admission charge.

Inland Seas Maritime Museum, 480 Main St., Vermilion, OH 44089. Ship models, artifacts, and relics of Great Lakes shipping. Daily, 10–5. Closed New Year's, Thanksgiving, and Christmas. Admission charge..

Oregon

Columbia River Maritime Museum, 1792 Marine Dr., Astoria, OR 97103. Light ship, small craft, nautical instruments and tools, ship models, artifacts, and relics of Great Lakes shipping. Daily, 10–5. Closed New Year's, Thanksgiving, and Christmas. Admission charge.

Pennsylvania

Flagship Niagara, 164 E. Front St., Erie, PA 16507. Historic U.S. brig *Niagara*, exhibits and naval architecture. June–Sept., Tues.–Sat., 9–5; Sun, 12–5. Closed major holidays. Admission charge.

Philadelphia Maritime Museum, 321 Chestnut St., Philadelphia, PA 19106-2779. Ship models, historic crafts, figureheads, paintings, weapons, memorabilia, and artifacts relating to shops and the sea. Tues.–Sat., 10–5; Sun., 1–5. Closed New Year's Eve and Day, Easter, Thanksgiving, Christmas Eve and Day. Admission charge.

Rhode Island

Herreshoff Marine Museum/America's Cup Hall of Fame, 7 Burnside St., Bristol, R.I. 02809. Forty sail and power yachts built at Herreshoff shipyard and America's Cup memorabilia. May–Oct., Mon.–Fri., 1–4; Sat. and Sun., 11–4. Closed Independence Day. Admission charge.

Museum at Yachting, Fort Adams State Park, Newport, RI 02840. Local yachts, America's Cup races, and a small boat collection. Mid-May–Oct., daily, 10–5. Admission charge.

Naval War College Museum, Naval War College, Coasters

Harbor Island, Newport, RI 02841-5010. In historic 1820 Founders Hall are art, artifacts, imprints, and prints on the history of naval warfare and Narragansett Bay naval heritage. Weekdays, 10–4; Sat.–Sun, 12–4. No charge.

Texas

Texas Maritime Museum, 1202 Navigation Circle, Rockport, TX 78382. Nautical equipment, commercial fishing gear, shipbuilding tools. Tues.–Sat, 10–4; Sun., 1–4. Closed New Year's, Easter, Thanksgiving, Christmas week. Admission charge.

Virginia

Hampton Roads Naval Museum, 1 Waterside Dr., Norfolk, VA 23514. Naval artifacts, models, weapons, archaeology, shop memorabilia, naval uniforms. Call (804) 444-8971 for hours of operation. Closed New Year's Day, Thanksgiving, and Christmas. No charge.

The Mariners Museum, 100 Museum Dr., Newport News, VA 23606. "Age of Exploration" gallery, ship designs, miniature ships, Chesapeake Bay gallery, small craft, navigational instruments, ship equipment, whaling and fishing, sailors' handiwork, figureheads, and maritime arts. Daily, 10–5. Closed Christmas. Admission charge.

Portsmouth Museum, 420 High St., Portsmouth, VA 23704. 1915 Lightship, Portsmouth Naval Shipyard Museum exhibits maritime, history, and military arts center. Also children's museum, lightship and Coast Guard equipment, uniforms, period exhibits, ship models, uniforms, weapons, and the SS *Virginia*–also known as the *Merrimac*. Tues.–Sat., 10–5; Sun., 1–5. Closed New Year's Day, Thanksgiving, and Christmas. Admission charge.

Virginia Beach Maritime Museum, Inc./ Life-Saving Museum of Virginia, 24th St. and Atlantic Ave., Virginia Beach, VA 23451. In the 1903 Coast Guard Station are ship models, maritime artifacts, scrimshaw, uniforms, and art.

Memorial Day–Oct., Mon.–Sat., 10–5; Sun., 12–5; Oct.–Memorial Day, Tues.–Sun., 10–5. Closed New Year's Eve and Day, Thanksgiving, and Christmas. Admission charge.

Watermen's Museum, 309 Water St., Yorktown, VA 23690. Exhibits emphasize Chesapeake Bay seafood industry from prehistoric times to today. Children's museum. April–Dec., Tues.–Sat., 10–4; Sun., 1–4. Admission charge.

Washington

Center for Wooden Boats, 1010 Valley St., Seattle, WA 98109. Historic small craft, models, tools of the Pacific Northwest. Winter: Mon., Wed.–Sun, 12–6; summer: daily, 10–6. Closed Thanksgiving and Christmas. No charge.

Naval Undersea Museum, 610 Dowell St., Keyport, WA 98345-7610. Extensive exhibits on undersea technology. June–Sept., Tues.–Sun., 10–4. Closed New Year's Day, Thanksgiving, and Christmas. No charge.

Wisconsin

Door County Maritime Museum (at Gills Rock), Memorial Park, Gills Rock, WI 54210. Sailing, fishing, shipbuilding, local shipyards, and a lighthouse. July–Aug., daily, 10–4; Memorial Day, June, and Sept.–mid-Oct., Sat–Sun., 10–4. No charge.

Manitowoc Maritime Museum, 75 Maritime Dr., Manitowoc, WI 54220. Ship's tools, salvage, artifacts, lake schooners, recreational boats, and a reproduction of a 19th-century schooner midship section. May–Sept., daily, 9–8; Oct.–April, daily, 9–5. Admission charge.

SS *Meteor* Maritime Museum, Barker's Island, Superior, WI 54880. Collections housed in hull and quarters of the 1896 SS *Meteor*, last of the whaleback-boat models, shipbuilding, history, ship's gear. Sept.–Oct., Sat.-Sun., 10–5. Admission charge.

BIBLIOGRAPHY

Books

Anthony, Irving. *Down to the Seas in Ships* (Philadelphia: The Penn Publishing Co., 1924).

Asley, Clifford W. *The Ashley Book of Knots* (Garden City, New York: Doubleday, Doran & Co., Inc., 1944).

Baldwin, Hanson W. *Sea Fights and Shipwrecks* (New York: Hanover House, 1955).

Bedford, Captain F.G.D., R.N., C.B. *The Sailor's Pocket Book:* Sixth Edition (Portsmouth: Griffin & Co., 2, The Hard, 1890).

Blandford, Percy W. *Knots & Splices* (New York: ARC Books, Inc., 1965).

Bloomster, Edgar L. *Sailing and Small Craft Down the Ages*

Bowdich, Nathaniel, L.L.D. *The New American Practical Navigator:* Tenth New Stereoscope Edition (New York: E. & G. W. Blunt, Proprietors, No. 179, Water St., Corner of Burling Slip, 1837).

Brady, William, Sailing Master U.S.N. *The Kedge-Anchor; or Young Sailors' Assistant:* Third Edition (New York: Published by the Author, 1848).

Braynard, Frank O. *Famous American Ships* (New York: Hastings House Publishers, 1956, 1978).

Brewington, M. V. *Chesapeake Bay: A Pictorial Maritime History* (Cambridge, Maryland: Cornell Maritime Press, 1953).

Brouwer, Norman. *International Registry of Historic Ships* (Oswestry, England: Anthony Nelson, 1985).

Brown, Raymond Lamont. *Phantoms of the Sea* (New York: Taplinge Publishing Co., 1972).

Chapelle, Howard I. *The History of American Sailing Ships,* Museum of History and Technology of the United States National Museum (Washington: U.S. Govt. Printing Office, 1935).

————. *The National Watercraft Collection,* Museum of History and Technology of the United States National Museum (Washington: U.S. Govt. Printing Office, 1935).

————. *The Search for Speed Under Sail 1700–1855* (New York: W. W. Norton & Company, Inc., 1967).

Chapman, Charles F., M.E. *Piloting Seamanship and Small Boat Handling,* Vol. V, Motor Boating's Ideal Series (New York: Published by Motor Boating, 572 Madison Avenue, 3rd Printing, 1943 edition).

Chatterton, E. Keble. *Seamen All* (Philadelphia: J. B. Lippincott Co., 1924; London: Sidwick and Jackson Limited, 1924).

————. *Ships & Ways of Other Days* (Philadelphia: J. B. Lippincott Co., 1913; London: Sidwick and Jackson Limited, 1913).

Clark, Hyla M. *The Tall Ships* (New York: Published in Association with Operation Sail, A Tree Communications/Alexis Gregory Book, 1976).

Culver, Henry B. *Forty Famous Ships* (Garden City, New York: Doubleday, Doran & Co., Inc., 1936).

Cutler, Carl C. *Grayhounds of the Sea* (New York & London: G. P. Putnam's Sons, 1930).

Dana, Richard Henry, Jr. *The Seaman's Friend* (Boston: Charles C. Little & James Brown & Benjamin Loring & Co., 1842; New York: Dayton & Saxton, and E. & G. W. Blunt, 1842; Philadelphia: Cary & Hart, 1842).

————. *Two Years Before the Mast* (Los Angeles: The Ward Richie Press, Vol. I and II, 1964).

Davis, Charles G. *Ships of the Past* (Salem, Mass.: Publication #19 of the Marine Research Society, Southworth Press, 1929).

————. *Ships of the Past* (Salem, Mass.: The Marine Research Society, The Southworth Press, Portland Maine, 1929).

Derby, W. L. A. *The Tall Ships Pass* (Camden, Maine: National Marine Publishing Co., 1937, 1970).

Eastman, Ralph M. *Yankee Ship Sailing Cards* (Boston, Mass.: Issued by State Street Trust Co., 1948).

Forbes, Allan. *Yankee Ship Sailing Cards* (Boston, Mass.: Issued by State Street Trust Co., 1948).

Ford, Norman D. "Ship Lace" (Greenlawn, New York: Havian Publications, 1953).

Gatty, Harold. *The Raft Book* (New York: George Grady Press, 445 West 41st Street, 1943).

Gibson, Charles E. *Handbook of Knots and Splices* (New York: Emerson Books, Inc., 1961, 1963).

Grafton, John. *New York in the Nineteenth Century* (New York: Dover Publications, Inc., 1977).

Grimwood, V. R. *American Ship Models and How to Build Them* (New York: Norton & Co., Inc., 1942).

Harlow, Frederick Pease. *The Making of a Sailor* (Salem, Mass.: Marine Research Society, 1928).

Haws, Duncan. *Ships and the Sea* (Thomas Y. Crowell Co., Inc., n.d.).

Hohman, Elmo Paul. *The American Whaleman* (New York: Longmans, Green & Co., 1928).

Hurst, Alex. A. (introduction by) *The Medley of Mast and Sail II* (Annapolis, Maryland: Naval Institute Press, 1981).

Johnson, Captain Irving. *Round the Horn in a Square Rigger* (Springfield, Mass.: Milton Bradley Co., 1932).

Kipping, Robert, N.A. *Sails and Sailmaking,* 14th Edition (London: Crosby Lockwood & Son, 1898; New York: Divan Nostrand Co., 1898).

Landstrom, Bjorn. *The Ship* (Garden City, New York: Doubleday & Co., Inc., 1961).

Leitch, Michael. *The Romance of Sail* (London: Hamlyn, 1975).

Lever, Darey. *The Young Sea Officer's Sheet Anchor or a Key to the Leading of the Rigging and to Practical Seamanship,* American Edition (New York: E. & G. W. Blunt, 1858).

Lewis, Edward V., and O'Brien, Robert. *Ships* (New York: Time–Life Books, 1965, 1970).

Lovette, Lieutenant Commander Leland P. USN. *Naval Customs, Traditions and Usage* (Annapolis, Maryland: United States Naval Institute, 1939; Menasha, Wisconsin: George Banta Publishing Company, 1939).

Mannix, Daniel P., and Cowley, Malcolm. *Black Cargoes* (New York: The Viking Press, 1962).

The Marine Room of the Peabody Museum of Salem (Salem, Mass.: Peabody Museum, Nichols Press, Lynn, 1921).

The Mariner's Pocketbook, 1st Edition (Scranton: International Correspondence Schools, Printed in the United States, 1906).

McCulloch, John Herries. *A Million Miles in Sail* (New York: Dodd, Mead & Co., 1933).

McCutchan, Philip, *Tall Ship* (New York: Crown Publishers, Inc., 1976).

McKay, Richard C. *Some Famous Sailing Ships of New England*, series two, Maritime Research Society (New York–London: G. P. Putnam's Sons, 1928).

McLanathan, Richard B.K. "Ship Models" (Connecticut: Meriden Gravure, Co., 1957).

Maury, M.F. L.L.D. Lieut. U.S. Navy. *The Physical Geography of the Sea*, Second Edition (New York: Harper & Brothers, Publishers, 329 & 331 Pearl St., Franklin Square, 1855).

Mixter, George W. *Primer of Navigation*, Sixth Edition (New York: Van Nostrand Reinhold Company, 1979).

Nares, George S., Lieut. R.N. *The Naval Cadet's Guide or Seaman's Companion* (Portsea: James Griffin, 82 Queen Street, 1860; London: Longman, Green, Longman, and Roberts, 1860).

Neider, Charles. *Great Shipwrecks and Castaways* (New York: Harper & Brothers, Publishers, 1952).

Parsons, Usher, M.D. *Sailor's Physician, Exhibiting the Symptoms, Causes and Treatment of Diseases Incident to Seamen and Passengers* (Cambridge: Printed by Hilliard & Metcalf, 1820).

Peters, Harry T. *Currier & Ives* (Garden City, New York: Doubleday, Doran & Co., Inc., 1942).

Pope-Hennessy, James. *Sins of the Fathers: A Study of the Atlantic Slave Traders 1441–1807* (New York: Alfred A. Knopf, 1968).

Puddington, Henry. *The Sailor's Horn-Book for the Law of Storms*, second edition (London: 1851).

Rawley, James A. *The Transatlantic Slave Trade* (New York–London: W. W. Norton & Co., 1981).

Regan, Paul M. Lieut. Commander, & Johnson, Paul H., Librarian, U.S. Coast Guard Academy. *Eagle Seamanship: A Manual for Square-Rigger Sailing* (Annapolis, Maryland: Naval Institute Press, 1979).

Robinson, John. *Old-Time Nautical Instruments* (Boston, Mass.: 1921).

The Marine Room of the Peabody Museum of Salem (Salem, Mass.: Peabody Museum, The Nichols Press, Lynn, 1921).

Robinson, John, and Dow, George Francis. *The Sailing Ships of New England*, Series Two (Salem, Mass.: Maritime Research Society, Southworth Press, Portland, Maine, 1924).

Rogers, Stanley. *The Sailing Ship* (New York: Harper & Brothers, 1950).

Rowe, William Hutchinson. *The Maritime History of Maine* (New York: W. W. Norton & Co., Inc., 1948).

Sawyer, Edmund Ogden, Jr. *Our Sea Saga: The Wood Wind Ships* (San Francisco: 1929).

Seamanship, Both in Theory and Practice (Newburyport: Edward Little and Co., Booksellers, May, 1811; Boston: E. Little, No. 8, State Street, Printed and sold by Edmund M. Blunt at his Nautical Book Store, Sign of the Quadrant, No. 202, Water-Street, Corner of Beckman-Slip, May, 1811).

Severy, Merle. *Men, Ships & the Sea* (Washington, D.C.: Prepared by National Geographic Book Service, National Geographic Society, 1962).

Smith, Hervey Garrett. *The Small-Boat Sailor's Bible* (Garden City, New York: Doubleday & Co., Inc., 1964).

Steel, David. *The Elements and Practice of Rigging and Seamanship*, 2 vols. (Little Tower Hill, Maryland: CC XCIV, printed for David Steel, Union Row).

The Seaman's Daily Assistant Containing Plane, Traverse, Parallel, Middle Latitude, and Mercator's Sailing with All the Necessary Tables and Rules for Working a Day's Work: Taken from the Works of Robertson, Mackay, Moore and Worie. (New York: Printed and published by William Elliot [Printer of the Nautical Almanac], Sign of the Ledger, 114 Water-Street, 1810).

Todd, John, and Whall, W. B. *Practical Seamanship for Use in the Merchant Service* (New York: John Wiley & Sons, 1890).

Tryekare, Tre. *The Lore of Ships* (New York: Crescent Books, 1972).

Villiers, Alan. *Give Me a Ship to Sail* (New York: Charles Scribner's Sons, 1953).

———. *The Way of a Ship* (New York: Charles Scribner's Sons, 1953).

Wallace, Frederick William. *Wooden Ships and Iron Men* (London: Hodder and Stoughton, Ltd., 1932).

Williams, Guy R. *The World of Model Ships and Boats* (New Jersey: Chartwell Books, Inc., 1971).

Wilson-Barker, Captain D., R.D., R.N.R. *Things a Sailor Needs to Know* (London: Charles Griffin and Company, Limited, 1918; Philadelphia: J. B. Lippincott Co., 1918).

American Sail Training Pamphlets

1. "Lake Ontario Tall Ships Rendezvous '84."
2. "The History of the International Sail Training Races" (n.d.).
3. Warburton, Barclay H. III, "Sail Training and the 'Tall Ships' Races," © 1975.
4. Richardson, Nancy Hughes (editor), "Sail Training Ships and Programs, 1985 Directory."
5. "Eagle." Photography by Robert de Gast. United States Naval Institute Proceedings Reprint Feb. 1970 Vol. 96 No. 2/804.

Articles

1. Berton, Pierre. "The Franklin Mystery," in *My Country: The Remarkable Past* (Seal Books, McClelland and Stewart, Bantam Limited Toronto [n.d.]).
2. Mooney, Michael J. "København is missing!" in *The Compass* (1984, No. 2, Vol. L 1x).
3. *Smithsonian* 16: 116–129 June 1985 (? author & title. About Franklin Expedition).
4. Wylie, Evan McLead. "Race to Terror" p. 66–69, p. 104–11 (concerning the "Marques"), in *Yankee*, May 1985.

Seafarers' viewpoints from:

George W. Crowninshield, president of American Sail Training Association

Elise Feeley, research librarian, Forbes Library, Northampton, Massachusetts

Boatswain's Mate David Kinner, U.S.C.G.

Captain Irving Johnson of the "Peking" and "Yankee."

Kirsten Mann, American Sail Training Association

Nancy Hughes Richardson, editor, 1985 Directory Sail Training Ships, Girl Scout Mariners

Commissioned Warrant Officer Richard T. "Red" Shannon

INDEX

Page numbers in italic indicate illustrations.